MW00683126

CHANCE

CHANCE ❧ ANNE METIKOSH

NeWest Press

Copyright © Anne Metikosh 2008

All rights reserved. The use of any part of this publication reproduced, transmitted in any form or by any means, electronic, mechanical, recording or otherwise, or stored in a retrieval system, without the prior consent of the publisher is an infringement of the copyright law. In the case of photocopying or other reprographic copying of the material, a licence must be obtained from Access Copyright before proceeding.

Library and Archives Canada Cataloguing in Publication

Metikosh, Anne, 1954-
Chance / Anne Metikosh.
ISBN 978-1-897126-20-2

1. Metikosh, Dragan. 2. Metikosh, Galina. 3. World War,
1939-1945--Biography. 4. Refugees--Europe--Biography. I. Title.

D811.5.M419 2008   940.53'1610922   C2007-906073-0

Editor for the Board: Michael Penny
Text editor: Carol Berger
Cover and interior design: Natalie Olsen
Cover image: Natalie Olsen
Author photo: Kate Metikosh

NeWest Press acknowledges the support of the Canada Council for the Arts, the Alberta Foundation for the Arts, and the Edmonton Arts Council for our publishing program. We also acknowledge the financial support of the Government of Canada through the Book Publishing Industry Development Program (BPIDP).

NeWest Press
201–8540–109 Street
Edmonton, Alberta T6G 1E6
(780) 432-9427
newestpress.com

No bison were harmed in the making of this book.
We are committed to protecting the environment and to the responsible use of natural resources. This book is printed on 100% recycled, ancient forest-friendly paper.

1 2 3 4 5 11 10 09 08   printed and bound in Canada

For the family,
past, present, and future

Serbian Family Tree

Metikoš

8 daughters   Gligo o- -
Fate unknown   (1879 – 1944)

Šesto

Mileva
(1879 – 1973)

Dragutin
(1882 – 1970)

Milan
(1903 – 1980)

Ankica
(1912 – 1988)

Vlado
(1914 – 2001)

Dragica
(1913 – 1993)

Milica
(1919 – 1997)

Dragan
(1920 –)

Russian Family Tree

Ivanov

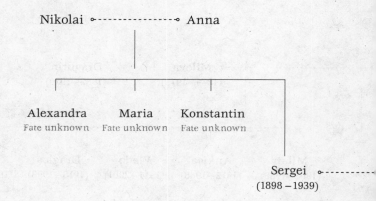

Nikolai o----------------o Anna

Alexandra   Maria   Konstantin
Fate unknown Fate unknown Fate unknown

Sergei o-----------
(1898 – 1939)

Ustinovich

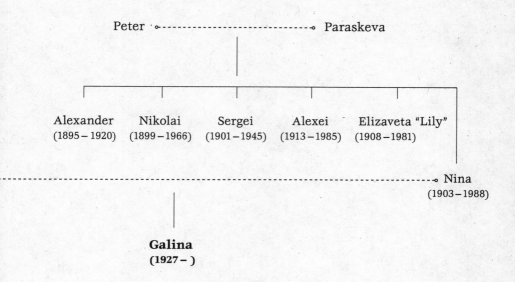

Peter o----------------------------------o Paraskeva

Alexander   Nikolai   Sergei   Alexei   Elizaveta "Lily"
(1895 – 1920)   (1899 – 1966)   (1901 – 1945)   (1913 – 1985)   (1908 – 1981)

Nina
(1903 – 1988)

Galina
(1927 –)

AUTHOR'S NOTE

The War years were many things to many people. There is incredible variety to be found in the interpretation of events that might, at first glance, seem clearly defined. The victor traditionally writes the official version of what happened but, seen through another lens, the same story can have a very different beginning, middle, and end. The tales historians tell us are based on documents, statistics, and dispatches. But the past is much more than official records—it is the lived experience of individuals.

Chance is a personal account of war, its prelude, and its aftermath. In novelizing my in-laws' lives I have, necessarily, imagined the details of certain scenes and conversations. For convenience, I have made composites of some secondary characters. But, essentially, what happens in *Chance* happened in real life, and Dragan and Galina's reflections on the past are an intimate view of the extraordinary times in which they lived. I am grateful to them for sharing their memories with me.

Memories colour all our perceptions. New experiences percolate through the old, gathering a hint of flavour as they pass. The fact that memory is unique to each of us was brought home to me after the death of my father earlier this year. Leafing through old photo albums, my brothers and I played a game of "Do you remember?" and found that sometimes not all of us did, and often in not quite the same way.

Memory is both ephemeral and enduring; it is our personal archive. Memory helps make us who we are. And more, it helps us hold on to those we love.

Anne Metikosh   Calgary, October 2007

xviii

Estonia

Latvia

Lithuania

Baltic Sea

Poland

Berlin

Essen
Ludwigshütte
Wetzlar

Germany

Czechoslovakia

Carpathian
Mountains

Austria

Hungary

Alps

Maribor

Romania

Zagreb

Petrinja

Belgrade

Yugoslavia

Adriatic
Sea

Bulgaria

Italy

Albania

Greece

Aegean
Sea

Dragan's journey

Galina's journey

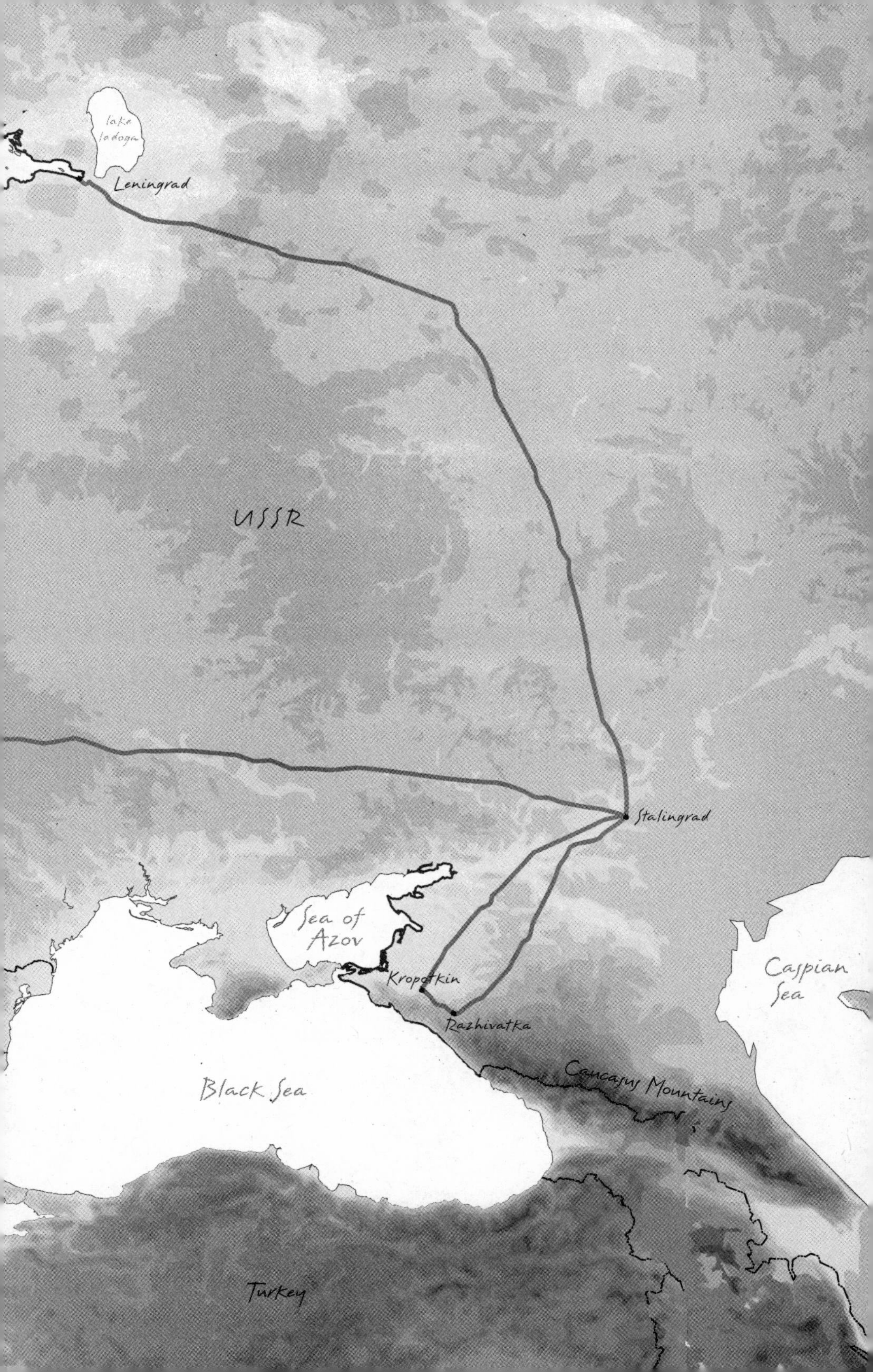

Lake
Ladoga

Leningrad

USSR

Stalingrad

Sea of
Azov

Kropotkin

Razhivatka

Caucasus Mountains

Caspian
Sea

Black Sea

Turkey

Men's lives are chains of chances
And history their sum.

— Bayard Taylor, man of letters

The only safe explanation is that things happen because they happen.

—A.J.P. Taylor, historian

FOREWORD

For more than eight hundred years the town of Wetzlar has prospered quietly on the banks of the Lahn River. Two world wars left it virtually untouched, so its Old Quarter looks almost the same at the dawn of the twenty-first century as it did in the days of Goethe. Steep cobblestone streets still wind their way up to the Dom that towers over the marketplace. Begun in the twelfth century and never really completed, so many different styles have been incorporated into the building of this cathedral that it stands as testament to the history of German ecclesiastical architecture. Lining the narrow roads of the town that surrounds it are half-timbered houses in styles ranging from Gothic to Baroque. Lace curtains hang in the windows. From time to time, the curtains twitch as the people behind them monitor what is happening in the street below.

On June 12, 1946, curtains were twitching in all the houses surrounding the main square. Behind them, shadowy figures peered out at the patch of dispirited grass where a small wedding party had assembled for a photograph. The great oak in the middle of the square partially blocked their view, but the uninvited guests still witnessed what was happening. Two more of the dispossessed had crossed the thirteenth-century *Lahnbrücke* from the refugee camp on the other side to register their marriage at the Stadtsamt.

It was not the stylish wedding of a young girl's dreams. There were no flowers, other than the small spray embroidered on the bride's dress, no candles, no organ playing, no priest in flowing raiment to bless the couple. Even the wellwishers were few: her mother to support the bride, whose father had long ago been swallowed in the maw of Stalin's gulag; a friend to stand with the groom. The bride's wedding dress was not elegant white silk, but simple navy cotton. The groom saw it before she did: he had grabbed it from a donation box in the relief office where he worked.

He signed the register with a flourish: Dragan Metikos. The bride's signature was more tentative. Years later, when they were safely in Canada, she would have the licence amended to her real name. But for now, let officials believe she was Alina Jankowska from Poland, not Galina Ivanova from Russia.

It had been a year since the Liberation and all over Europe refugees were packing their bags. Some made their way home to seek out lost relatives and sift through the wreckage of bomb blast and shellfire, in a frantic attempt to recover the past. Those with nothing left to salvage carved new lives wherever the maelstrom spit them out. Many bought passage to North America, putting an ocean between them and devastation. But for millions of others, there were no options. Their fate had been decided at Yalta: all Russians would return to their Soviet homeland. They would be repatriated. By force, if need be.

When Germany surrendered to the Allies, nearly six million Russians were stranded in Western Europe. Some had been imported by the Nazis as slave labour. Some were prisoners of war. Some were anti-Communists fighting in German uniform. Many were women and children. Three million of them sheltered in territories occupied by the Western Allies, and they were prepared to pay any price to avoid returning to Russia. They knew what awaited them there. The Soviets considered them traitors. On their return, they would be shot or shipped to Siberia.

In the aftermath of war and faced with the menace of Yalta, countless Russians and Estonians, Latvians, and Lithuanians were sent home. They were driven aboard transports like animals, prodded by the bayonets of British and American soldiers who, just months before, had been their allies. In hopeless protest thousands hanged themselves, fell on their pocket knives, flung themselves under the moving wheels of railway cars, or cut their throats with rusty razor blades — anything not to face the Soviet concentration camps, torture, and death.

At DP Centre 538 in Wetzlar, the displaced stared with desperate eyes from behind gated enclosures where they waited for the cattle cars to take them east. Absent from the group was Galina Sergeyvna Ivanova, born in Leningrad, living under an assumed name in a camp where a converted pigsty was her home. Teenager, refugee, bride.

As she took the arm of her new husband, Galina was aware of the twitching curtains in the windows surrounding the square, and of the staring eyes. She found the curiosity oppressive. It enhanced the sense of loss and rude awakening she had felt when she signed her marriage certificate.

Galina was born during the iron years, when Russian revolutionary mills ground ever more harshly, crushing all opposition, both real and imagined. She grew up dreaming of a golden era she read about in novels, her imagination full of horse-drawn sleighs in white snow and warm summer evenings in leafy parks. Losing herself in the words of Tolstoy, the music of Tchaikovsky, and the dancing feet of Ulunova, she could ignore the leitmotif of paranoia that underscored her life. But the lovely nineteen-year-old with the braided coronet of brown hair and a string of eager suitors was now a wife. The romantic dreams were over. Like a sleeping princess, she awoke to reality with a kiss from her prince.

Dragan thought Galina the most beautiful girl he had ever seen. From the moment they met, winning her became his obsession. She was the candy in the store window, the prize to redeem all the losses of the previous four years. With so many rivals for her attention, the young Serb had no scruples about how he would win his Russian doll. And so began the daily visits to her mother, Nina, the generous bribes of cigarettes and coffee, and his education in the realities of Soviet life.

As a student in Yugoslavia, Dragan, like many of his friends, had flirted with the ideals of Communism. When the war ended, Tito's partisans were firmly in control and Dragan thought he would go home to gain what benefit he could from the new regime. He didn't know that his family had already held a memorial for him or that his name was inscribed at the local school on a plaque honouring the dead. He wanted to marry Galina and take her home to show her off. Nina rejected the plan. They had finally escaped Communist tyranny; Nina wouldn't sanction a return to it. Negotiation ensued, and she and Dragan struck a deal. If Galina rejected him, Dragan would go back to Yugoslavia alone. If she agreed to marry him, he would take them all to Canada.

Only one photograph was taken of Dragan and Galina's wedding and by a quirk of fate, one of the key players was nearly cut from the picture; only an arm shows. For years, with the photograph lying somewhere in a shoebox, Galina was sure that she was the missing person; that the photographer had accurately recorded her flight reaction to her newly wedded state. In fact, she is the one in the centre of the picture, supported by the arm of an invisible husband.

Dragan and Galina have now been married sixty years. A Serb and a Russian, ancient allies. In 1948 they abandoned Camp 538 and the devastation of Europe with thirteen dollars, a few belongings, and even fewer words of English between them. The emotional baggage they carried was much heavier.

NO PICNIC

Yugoslavia, 1926

❧

I have heard many stories about my childhood, but they are not very important. What matters is that I survived all the illnesses of childhood and all the situations that came after that were difficult and dangerous and many times life-threatening. I have survived all of them and I am able to talk about them now, even in my broken English. Some things I remember quite vividly. Others, I only think I know.
   — Dragan

"We'd be better off if the boy died."

   Six-year-old Dragan was used to hearing the words. His mother recited them daily when she struggled to divide a meagre supper into eight portions. But this was the first time they had come at the end of a nearly inaudible prayer, delivered as she knelt in the grass before a ragged line of crosses. On his knees beside her, Dragan peered up at his mother from behind an untidy fringe of brown hair. Something fluttered in his stomach as he stared at her. Her vivid blue eyes were also his and they shared the same straight nose and wide mouth, but Dragan had never seen his mother's thin lips smile. Her pallid cheeks had always been etched with the lines of suffering and fatigue.

   When they had set off that morning, the boy's thin body was

vibrating with excitement. The tall wooden crosses that adorned the hill behind the village had fascinated him since that day a year before, when he watched a procession wind its way past his house and up the grassy slope. A bearded priest in flowing black robes led the way. Behind him four men, Dragan's father among them, struggled to support the long, heavy box on their shoulders. They were flanked by others with standards bearing the bright banners of the church and followed by half the village. The flags snapped in the breeze so that embroidered icons of saints and crosses fluttered above the heads of the people. Dragan's heart beat faster at the sight. He wondered about the body in the box. What would happen to it once it was placed in the ground? Did the spirits of the people on the hill wander among the crosses? Did they speak through the carvings in the wood? He was finally going to find out.

His mother had been up the hill a few weeks before. Dragan had watched her pack a few carefully measured seeds into the pocket of her apron. But though he waited eagerly by the door, she affected not to see him and so he did not follow her. Today she hesitated, wondering if the spindly legs of her youngest and frailest child could carry him up the hill and back. The boy had the wistful look of a puppy about to be left behind. When she grudgingly nodded at him, Dragan jumped up with the same graceless, incredulous pleasure of the puppy that is being taken for a walk after all.

It was a sunny day a month past Easter, and the green-gold of vines wound fragile tendrils through the deepening pink of the cherry trees at the gate. As they climbed, the familiar clang of milk cans, the jangle of horse harness, and the shouts of neighbour greeting neighbour faded until all Dragan could hear was his own rasping breath and, high overhead, the faint cry of a bird. He stopped and shaded his eyes against the sun for a better look at the three black shapes that circled on motionless wings.

But they were too far away for Dragan to tell if they were hawks or merely crows. He studied them long enough for his breathing to return to normal, then followed his mother the rest of the way up the hill.

By the time he caught up to her, she was on her knees before a small group of crosses. Dragan could see the shoots of the primroses she had planted earlier already pushing through the earth around them.

There was no one else on the hill. The ghosts that Dragan had imagined were silent. No spirits hovered. With the sun now high overhead, even the shadows had fled. It was, after all, only a burial yard. All that remained were bones. Dragan had seen bones before: animal carcasses scattered in the fields, skeletons picked clean by scavengers and bleached white by the sun. He wondered if these bones would be different, hidden away like guilty secrets, with no light to polish them and only worms for company. But then, blanketed as they were in their boxes, perhaps they felt as cozy as he did when he curled up to sleep in the nook cut into the wall beside the big stone fireplace his father had built.

Dragan watched his mother's rough, reddened hands work the earth below the crosses carved to the memory of his unknown brothers and sisters. He mimicked her actions in the dirt beneath the one inscribed with his own name, Dragutin, knowing he had been christened less in honour of one lost than in the hope he might follow him to an early grave. He stole another look at his mother's impassive face, wondering if she had loved her lost children, wondering if she loved him. Thinking about it always gave him an awful, anxious feeling in the pit of his stomach. So he tried not to think about it much.

"It would be better if the boy died."

There was no malice in Mileva's words. After bearing twelve children and burying half of them, she was tired. A lifetime of labour had netted her three sons, three daughters, six crosses, and a red-tiled roof. It sat oddly on the stone and plank dwelling that was their home, where the family sheltered in two rooms beneath it and livestock lowed in the barn beneath them. Mileva's husband Gligo was proud of that roof. He had earned it piece by piece during the years he had worked on the other side of the world, in Chicago. The strapping six-foot-two Gligo had left the house and an infant son in the capable hands of his diminutive wife while he set off for the country where jobs were said to be plentiful. He had returned five years later with enough money for the roof.

It became a landmark in Bijele Vode, one among the thousands of Balkan villages whose peasantry had sent their children to war against foreign invaders for centuries as great powers competed for empire across them. Perched on the edge of starvation, these villages had suffered the rise and fall of Greeks, Romans, Bulgars, Serbs, Turks, and Austro-Hungarians. In their churches, Orthodox had broken painfully from Catholic and both had battled Islam. Each new episode of history added to a pattern of slaughter and suppression that divided families and fostered grudges until the Balkan people could agree on neither politics nor religion. After the Great War, a loose Kingdom of South Slavs was cobbled together, but the stitches holding it were frayed from the outset.

While the 1920s roared in the rest of the western world, eighty percent of Yugoslavia's population still scratched out a living in the same manner as the Metikos family. Gligo tended his livestock, his hayfield, and his vineyard. He made gallons of *rakija* and *slivovitz* and sold for profit what he didn't drink. Unhappily for his fortune, he drank quite a lot. At least it took the edge off his temper.

The family's hand-to-mouth existence left no room for slackers. Children were put to work early, and before he started school, Dragan was in charge of feeding the chickens and harvesting

4

sunflower seeds. When he was six, Mileva said, "Dragi, you're old enough to tend the geese."

The boy's narrow chest swelled with the new responsibility. He enjoyed overseeing his little flock. He felt taller each time he successfully rounded them up and herded them back through the gate to the night-time safety of the farmyard. And if the occupation often left him alone, out of sight of the house, out of call of his parents, it taught him to enjoy solitude.

There were times, though, when emptiness pressed a little too closely, when leaf rustle and animal cry cast a spell that sent spiders of apprehension scurrying down his spine. Then his hand reached automatically into his pocket for his most treasured possession: his harmonica. It was the only gift he had ever received from his mother. Away from his family's critical ears, he taught himself to play, discovering notes with the same sense of anticipation explorers felt when they set out for new worlds. Like a miniature Pan, he sat under a tree surveying his flock, and piped away fear.

Calamity struck the day he left the harmonica at home. It was late August, a still, sultry day, when Mileva told Dragan he was to take the flock to forage on the remains of their neighbour Macek's cornfield. It would be the furthest he had ever been from home and his cousin Ilija was to go with him. Dragan was reluctant to expose his amateur musical skill, so he left the harmonica at home, folded carefully into his Sunday shirt. Now he wished he had it close at hand, for use as a weapon against the fat, hissing creature that was staring him down with such malevolent eyes.

That morning the enemy had been an ordinary gander, arrogant and bad-tempered like all ganders, but manageable. Dragan and his cousin Ilija had stumped along behind the dozen geese in their care, driving them forward with little shouts of *"hah"* and taps of a stick on the backs of the stragglers. Ilija was strong and stocky, with an unruly shock of dark brown hair. Beside him, Dragan looked paler and thinner than ever. Even so, since the geese belonged to Mileva, her son was nominally in charge of them as he and Ilija drove them to forage. The birds had padded docilely over sunburned hills as though they knew what awaited them and felt it was worth the journey. Led by the gander, the geese broke into an awkward, web-footed trot when they finally spied the scattered remains of the newly harvested field. Having reached it, the birds waddled contentedly for hours among the stalks, devouring the juicy kernels of grain with little gobbles of satisfaction. By mid-afternoon, they were dazed and dizzy from their feast and offered no resistance when Dragan and Ilija rounded them up, shooing them back towards home.

The sun was high, the air still and close. Sweat gathered at the nape of Dragan's neck and pooled in the crooks of his elbows. Dry grass crackled under his bare feet. His mind leaped ahead to the creek that ran across the bottom of their yard, but the corn-bloated flock resisted his demands for more speed until the water was actually in view. When they finally reached it, the birds paddled blissfully in the ripples, while Dragan and Ilija abandoned the job of gooseherds for the joys of wading and splashing, cupping their hands to let cool, clear water trickle down parched throats. After their swim, the geese decided on a nap in the long grass of the creek bank. Ilija hunted tadpoles. Dragan followed the flock's example and threw himself under the shade of a chestnut tree.

His timing was unfortunate because the big grey gander had not yet settled himself. He was still casting about for the most comfortable spot to rest his regal feathers when Dragan's sigh of bliss attracted his attention. Slowly, the gander waddled over and suggested with a low-pitched honk that Dragan should move. Drugged by the heat and the soporific drone of bees among the sunflowers, Dragan waved his hand to shoo the bird away. The gander responded with a menacing flap of its wings. Startled, Dragan sat up and was appalled to see the gander not three feet away. Fat with corn, long neck arching, the bird looked bigger than the boy. Dragan opened his eyes very wide then squinted them very small, screwing his face into a terrible grimace in an effort to scare off his attacker. The gander emitted an evil hiss and took two steps forward.

Stomach churning, Dragan cast about for a twig, a leafy branch, any weapon with which to repel attack. His fingers closed on a stone and in desperation he hurled it as hard as he could and scrambled to his feet to confront the enemy.

The gander collapsed.

Dragan rushed over for a closer look at the motionless bird. The heavy body lay still, legs poking stiffly out from the feathered belly, a trickle of blood on its head. The bottom fell out of Dragan's world.

The slaughter of animals for food was routine. But what lay before him was no ordinary goose fattened for the dinner table. This was the linchpin of the flock. Killing it meant, at the very least, a beating. His first thought was to conceal the evidence of his crime. Dragan scooped the limp body into his arms and threw it into the creek. He cast a terrified look at his cousin.

Ilija was already tearing up the slope toward the house, waving his arms and yelling for his aunt.

Dragan opened his mouth to call him back, but a noisy splash made him spin around to see that the shock of cold water had miraculously revived the corpse. Dragan gasped and sent a quick prayer of thanks heavenward, but his relief quickly turned to frustration as the gander stubbornly refused to come back out of the water. All of the boy's exhortations fell on deaf ears. His arm-waving was to no avail. Wading into the creek to chase the bird out the other side, Dragan was humiliated by the look of scorn it gave him as it paddled out of reach.

From where he stood flapping his arms at the gander, Dragan could see the farmhouse. In the yard, his father and his brother

Vlado were loading sheep into the wagon, ready to take them to market. The commotion down at the creek had caught their attention and now they stood, one of the sheep half on, half off the wagon between them, mouths open in amazement at the scene below.

Meanwhile Ilija, in his haste to relay the news of the gander's murder, had not witnessed its revival. He reached the farmhouse door out of breath and panted out the story of Dragan's evil deed. Instantly, Mileva grabbed the willow switch she kept beside the door and marched purposefully toward the creek.

Halfway there she met Dragan, who had finally persuaded the gander to join the rest of the flock waddling up the hill. Heedless of her son's cries and blind to the evidence in front of her, Mileva swung the rod. Above the *thwack* of the stick and his mother's curses, Dragan heard his father's raucous laugh echo across the yard.

ii

More than twenty years before Dragan confronted the gander, his father — a tall, handsome only son, raised in a household of eight doting sisters — surprised the people of Bijele Vode by marrying the orphan daughter of an Austro-Hungarian gendarme.

Mileva was the eldest of three children born to Mihailo Sesto and his wife. She was six when her father was killed in an uprising in which Serb rebels fought to free their homeland from its Austro-Hungarian occupiers. Her mother died soon after, and as the law demanded, the orphaned children were repatriated to the village where their father had been born, to be raised by relatives they had never met. Dragutin, the boy, went to school. The girls stayed home to learn essential wifely skills: housekeeping, sewing, and animal husbandry. Mileva wanted more. Every night while Dragutin did his homework, she sat beside him, looking at his books and papers and peppering him with questions. Soon she became the only girl in Bijele Vode who could read and write.

She met Gligo at a haying party, where the girls in their dirndls on one side of the meadow eyed the barefoot young men on the other, and both sides mentally calculated the possibilities for a future spouse. Mileva, noting the size of Gligo's feet, burst out, "Who on earth would ever agree to knit socks that big?"

As things turned out, she did, for over forty years. No doubt there was some element of affection between the two young people, but Gligo, catch that he was himself, was also no fool and he recognized that in Mileva he had found a woman in a thousand: one who could knit, sew, weave, cook, sow crops and reap them, tend animals, children and in-laws, and who was, moreover, literate. Though the top of her head barely reached his shoulder and she had no family connections to recommend her, Gligo married her.

If there had been a photo of the wedding, little Dragan would not have recognized his mother in it. The faded old woman he knew bore no resemblance to the energetic, fresh-faced girl who married for better or for worse in 1903.

While Mileva struggled to put food on the table for her children, her brother Dragutin became an officer in the Austrian army and profited by the upheaval of the First World War to build himself a small fortune and then marry a minor countess. Conscious that he enjoyed advantages denied to his sisters, Dragutin took an active interest in the welfare of their families. And in the winter of 1928, genie-like, he produced a small sack of gold coins to pay school fees on the island of Lokrum for his nieces, Milica and Maria, and his youngest nephew, Dragan.

The first snow had fallen early, greying the fields, then turning them white as the drifts grew higher and the creek turned to ice. Tree limbs cracked with frost and outside the stable, piles of manure stained the whiteness like ink on a handkerchief. Dragan was eight and too small and thin to make his way through the snow to school, even if he had had boots to wear. The one pair of *opanci* assigned to him had been lost in an ill-advised creek crossing, before the ice was strong enough to support even Dragan's weight. The boots were mired firmly in the muck and would stay there until the creek bed thawed. Dragan remembered how blue his feet had been by the time he had stumbled into the house, and how red his cheek had turned under his father's hand. The bruise lingered for weeks.

Having been promoted from gooseherd to cow minder, Dragan spent the long months alternately wresting hay from the stacks in the loft below and sitting by the window with a battered copy of *Robinson Crusoe*. It took him most of the winter to get through it. Daylight hours were short and the cost of carbide too high to keep the lamps lit into the evening. Not until April were the roads clear enough for the trip to Lokrum.

Dragan expected his own adventure would be quite different from Crusoe's. He hungered for the sight of olive groves and lemon trees, the star-shaped fort on the headland of the island, and the monastery that housed the school he would attend. Best of all, part of the journey would be by train.

In an era when most Yugoslav peasants lived and died in the villages where they were born, boarding a train headed hundreds of miles west of Bijele Vode was a major exploit. Dragan didn't notice the hard seats or the dingy *coupé*. He didn't mind the teeth-rattling vibration as the train jarred and bounced across uneven intersections of ill-maintained track, so mesmerized was he by the passing scenery. The train moved slowly enough that he could take in every detail of the rolling countryside, bright with blossoms and the tender shoots of emerging vines. Mileva rested her head against the back of the seat, enjoying the respite from workaday routine. Her eyes were closed, either in prayer or sleep, against the intrusive enthusiasm of the children. The girls pointed and exclaimed over everything they saw. Dragan sat silent, his nose pressed against the window, his shoulders tense with excitement. They passed by villages as poor and dusty as Bijele Vode, and through entire towns of handsome red-roofed buildings until they reached the seaport of Split.

Dragan never blinked, he barely remembered even to breathe as the four of them, hands as firmly coupled as the cars on the train, threaded their way through crowds of important, well-dressed people, down narrow streets where vendors touted an endless array of wares, and past ancient churches dark with mystery and meaning.

Turning into the market square, they were met by a scream, a string of shouted oaths, and the excited barking of a dog. A wagon piled high with bags of feed careered out of control behind a pair of plunging horses. Black flanks loomed over Dragan as the great beasts shied, whinnying, and sparks flew as their iron-shod feet rang against the cobbles. Mileva yanked the children sharply out of the way. The driver spat and flourished his whip. The lash flicked in a quick, cracking arc across the back of the dog that had caused the panic and the horses were pulled to a sweating stop.

In the calm that followed, Mileva hustled her charges across the square and down a quiet alley that exited at a seafront lined with palms and a harbour alive with ships that scurried like beetles across it.

"There," said Mileva, pointing. The boat that would take them to Lokrum was anchored at the quay.

Half an hour later, Dragan stood on deck. He clutched the rail and watched in fascination as burly dockhands loosed thick restraining ropes and the boat moved slowly away from the dock, turning southward for its journey along the coast. Dragan swallowed hard. The tangy smell of salt water and the rush of wind in his face made his heart swell. Milica and Maria crowded close, laughing at the seagulls that dipped and screeched in the boat's frothing wake. Ahead, nestled in the protective arm of steep cliffs, a scattered archipelago of subtropical islands lay waiting.

Tiny Lokrum belonged to the sprawling red-tiled city of Dubrovnik. It owed its fame to a legend, that Richard the Lion-Hearted, on his way home to England from the Third Crusade, had been shipwrecked there. Grateful not to have ended his life at the bottom of the sea, Richard vowed to build a church as a gesture of thanksgiving. But the people of Dubrovnik felt that the city, rather than the island, should benefit from the king's largesse and they asked him to build a cathedral instead. He did. In turn, they established an abbey on Lokrum.

In the mid-1800s, Archduke Maximilian von Hapsburg bought the island and transformed the abbey into a luxurious villa. But he didn't have long to enjoy it: as Emperor of Mexico, he was assassinated just eight years later. Ownership of the abbey reverted to the government, which turned it into a school for those wealthy enough to afford it. As a democratic gesture, a few spots were reserved for those in special need. Three of those places were bought with the small sack of gold from Uncle Dragutin and careful budgeting meant enough coins in the bag to keep Dragan, Milica, and Maria on Lokrum for three years.

A farewell hug on the quay, a stern admonishment to good behaviour, and Mileva was gone. She wrote to her son perhaps twice in the next three years. What was there to for her to say? Life went on as it always had, her endless litany of everyday chores interrupted only by a gathering at the church or a visit from the priest. The idea of making another trip to Lokrum never crossed her mind.

Dragan was too busy to care. The Catholic nuns at the school tended the children well. There was plenty to eat, more fruit and vegetables than Dragan had seen in his lifetime, fresh fish and wholesome bread, and gradually the spindly little boy began to put on weight and grow strong. He didn't see much of his sister or his cousin at the school as boys and girls were strictly segregated except at mealtimes. Although their days were circumscribed by Catholic prayers and hymns, a bearded Orthodox priest came twice a week to help keep their ties to their own faith strong.

The island was an Eden of cypress groves, pine trees, and vineyards. Lemons and oranges, aromatic herbs, and flowers perfumed the air and succulents —palm, agaric, and cactus —gave it an exotic look. When he wasn't in the classroom, Dragan picked seeds from the sunflowers, learned to harvest olives, and helped the nuns make tomato sauce in the big kitchen. Though the island was liberally dotted with olive trees, one in particular caught Dragan's fancy. It grew just off the main path from the quay to the abbey, its wizened trunk twisted and scarred into fantastic shapes. Whenever Dragan passed it, he imagined mysterious, long-robed monks and heard the murmured whispers of their ancient Latin prayers.

In the southeast corner of the island was a small lake called Mrtvo More which linked to the open sea. Dragan first saw it in the morning light, when the tide was out and some of the seabed lay exposed. The children had been told that this was where they would swim. Dragan was intrigued but a little apprehensive. He didn't know how to swim. Splashing in the creek at home hardly qualified.

Wandering out onto the tidal flat, he felt the wet sand oozing between his toes and wondered what his mother would say about such a mess. He admired the shape of the lakebed stretched out before him. It was dotted with lumps of coral and strings of seaweed. Beyond it was the deepening blue of the sea. He laughed when water rushed to fill his footprints, creating tiny lakes where he walked. Further out, it washed over his feet and further still, it rose to his knees like warm bathwater. Under the watchful gaze of the nuns, children chased each other across the mud and searched for treasure between the rocks. Ignoring their shrieks of capture and discovery, Dragan pursued his single-minded course toward the sea. By the time he came level with a rocky outcropping crowned by a twisted cypress tree, the water was lapping at his waist. Dragan fixed on that spot. He could safely wade this far at ten in the morning. He assumed the same would be true at three in the afternoon.

After lunch, the nuns shepherded their charges back to the lake to swim and the tide had come fully in. Landmarks on the lake bottom had disappeared, coral and seaweed had vanished. Wavelets flirted with the eye, making depth impossible to judge. Still confident in his earlier calculations, Dragan made directly for his spot by the twisted cypress. He took two deep breaths to steady his nerves, then clasped his hands in front of him like a martyr facing lions, and jumped in.

His small body broke the surface with a resounding splash and kept on falling. Legs flailing, he tried to touch bottom with his feet, but bottom wasn't where it had been in the morning. Stretch as he might, he could find no way to both anchor himself to the lakebed and keep his head above water. Had he shrunk? He had only been wet to the knees before. Salt stung his eyes and when he opened his mouth to call for help, the sea rushed in there, too. Sharp limestone rocks that had been so easy to avoid in the morning ripped at his hands and feet as Dragan thrashed and churned his way back to the shore and safety.

Panting, he hauled himself out of the water. His careful planning had come to naught. Mrtvo More had played him false. And yet, for a moment or two he had felt as though he were floating. The weight of his body, slight though it was, had no longer bound him to earth. He wondered if swimming might not be worth another try. Perhaps if he splashed about less wildly and adopted the paddle that some of the others were using, he might have better results. It was certainly worth the chance.

THE SNOW MAIDEN

Leningrad, 1937

I really didn't feel much at the time. I suppose
I was too busy just trying to survive from one day
to the next. But now, at the other end of life,
I have more time to reflect on the past and it haunts me.
— Galina

On the day her father disappeared, Galina lay under an apple tree at her grandmother's dacha, happily munching a windfall as she painted castles in the sky. Leningrad was forty miles to the north and could have been four thousand for all she cared. She didn't miss the musty stench that wafted up the apartment stairwell from a basement that constantly flooded. She didn't yearn for the incessant rattle of streetcars outside her window or the snaking lineups outside the shops.

For as long as Galina could remember, summers had been spent in this simple wooden farmhouse near the forest. Every year, as daylight lengthened toward the long white nights of the solstice and the flowering jasmine and linden trees brought a holiday mood to the city, Galina impatiently awaited the train trip to the country. There she could listen to the rooster's crow, count the needles on the pines, and watch patterned clouds lazily drift across azure skies. She delighted in the feel of the sun as it slanted through the silvery leaves of the white-barked birch trees surrounding the cottage, and in the soft dust of the dirt road under her bare feet.

Summer was a time for grandmothers. Her mother's mother, Paraskeva, lived in Leningrad and it was she who took Galina on the train, then arranged for the wagon that would meet them on market day to take them to the cottage. They always arrived in Luga with a few days in hand. For those few days, Businka Paraskeva, with her long skirts and old-fashioned ways, handed over care of her granddaughter to Grandma Anna. Businka called her *komsomolotchka,* in mocking recognition of the younger woman's slavish attendance at Party rallies and seminars. Anna's short skirts and progressive manner grated on Paraskeva so much that she spent only the minimum time in polite enquiry as to health and well-being before taking herself off to visit friends until market day.

Galina found Anna slightly alarming. But one tradition they observed together in perfect communion was the *troitsa,* the planting of birch trees around the house in memory of loved ones who had died. In the lucky years, when no new trees were needed, ribbons were tied around the trunks of those already in the ground.

At Luga in high summer all the farmers' children were busy weeding vegetables and gathering the berries, mushrooms, and hazelnuts they sold to cottagers. Rent on their cottage was paid for in chores, which left Paraskeva little time for amusing a ten-year-old. Galina amused herself with fantasies, inhabiting a dream world peopled by swan-necked ballerinas and dying heroes. While most of her friends were still pondering the fate of *Kashtanka,* Chekhov's little lost dog, Galina surprised the librarian by requesting Knut Hampsun's romantic *Victoria. War and Peace* captivated her, too, though she did skip the battle scenes in her haste to discover the fate of the lovers, Natasha and Pierre.

At Luga, Galina liked to read under a tree. In Leningrad, she preferred to curl up in the big armchair in Grandfather Peter's study. Peter Ustinovich had printed his own books. Though the machinery had long ago been dismantled, and Grandfather himself was gone, the cloying smell of black ink lingered in the fabric of the room, and tidy stacks of magazines still tempted a young girl. Some of them dated back twenty years or more and Galina's favourites featured pictures of the tsar and tsarina who ruled Russia before the revolution.

Grandfather Peter had actually met the tsar once. He had been invited to the state apartments in the dazzling green and white Winter Palace. Nicholas II had stood at the end of a flowing red carpet, magnificent in his braided uniform and shining sword. He had smiled his regal smile and Peter had bowed his head humbly and accepted the medal his emperor awarded him. Paraskeva insisted that such a thing had never happened but Galina had seen the medal with her own eyes. She was certain that the Tsar would not have honoured her grandfather as a good citizen by sending it in the mail.

Galina sighed to think that the glory days were over. How wonderful it must have been to attend one of the great balls, to arrive in a carriage and have your gown rustle and swish as a footman helped you alight. She imagined her own waist-length hair piled high in shining brown curls, glittering sapphires around her neck reflecting the blue of her eyes. The revolution had put an end to such fantasies, toppled the tsar, divided the country, and plunged its people into a brutal civil war. She understood it as a chess game, the Red Army facing off against the White, the players sacrificing queens and castles, bishops, and pawns as they battled across the countryside.

Uncle Alexander, Peter's son, had been a Red. He had died long before Galina was born, but she knew her mother still mourned the loss of her adored older brother. How often had she heard the stories from her mother, her grandmother, her Aunt Lily? Alexander had had no time for tsars or medals. He championed a democratic Russia and in the days before the bloody terror, he joined the Bolsheviks, who fought for an elected parliament. Once they were in power, though, he was jailed for disagreeing with them on how they handled voting in the new government. The wholesale promotion of insiders into all the top jobs offended Alexander's understanding of the democratic ideal, and he said so. For this he was thrown into prison, where he contracted the tuberculosis that killed him.

Peter's second son, Serge, had movie star looks that turned Galina's friends weak at the knees. He aspired to medicine but the taint of his brother's censure extended to him. Under the Rule of Minus Nine, he was arrested and exiled. It was a funny name, Galina thought, and a funny rule that allowed an offender to live anywhere in Russia he pleased with the exception of nine cities, those being the nine largest. After the revolution, they also happened to be the only cities where one could buy bread, or shoes, or get an education. However, the government machine didn't yet function smoothly, and it took time for paperwork from the top to flow to the regional soviets. Uncle Serge turned the bureaucratic chaos to his advantage. He defied the Communists and attended a series of medical schools, one term here, one term there, always a step ahead of the local authority. It reminded Galina of a game of leapfrog. Of course, once Serge had qualified as a doctor, he became a valuable commodity. Then the Communists took advantage of him, at least until the Great Patriotic War began. Then they sent him to the front.

At school, Galina learned about the Glorious Revolution, about Lenin and Stalin and how they overthrew the tsar who had given her grandfather his medal. Comrade Stalin was a hero, with a hero's goal of turning a peasant economy, a country whose people still wore birchbark shoes, into a modern industrial power. The millions who laboured to build the new factories, highways, and dams that Stalin demanded were grateful to him for the joy in their daily lives. So the newspapers said, and the billboards and the movies produced at the Lenfilm Studios where Uncle Konstantin worked. He had recently produced a film called *Gay Young People,* highlighting the joie de vivre of Soviet youth and their accomplishments. Galina begged to be allowed to visit the studio where, maybe, she would meet the great Orlova, or even be offered a part in a film herself. Her father curtly said no.

"But why not, Papa?"

He gave her a look she knew only too well. Later she overheard him telling her mother, "I won't let Galya have anything to do with those people. I know he's my brother, but he named his own daughter Ninel, for heaven's sake. Just spell it backwards. The damned Bolsheviks have managed to turn even the cinema into a weapon — those bastards with their guns in one hand and their cameras in the other. Well, they can take all the credit they like for 'elevating' art to this new level. I don't want my daughter involved in it." It was a sentiment he dared not express outside their home.

Galina quietly put on the red scarf of the Young Pioneers every morning on her way to school, and as quietly took it off again before she walked in the door. Wearing it in front of her father was like waving a flag in front of a bull.

It was confusing trying to sort out who was right and who was wrong in Soviet Russia. Even history, which ought to be fixed in time and space, was regularly altered. At least once a month, Galina's teacher directed the class to paste new pages over old in their textbooks, effectively turning fact into a grand, serialized fiction.

The Planning Commission, Gosplan, repeatedly drew up five-year plans that decided every detail of every branch of economic activity. Since the state was the only employer, all workers became de facto slaves of the plan. Every enterprise and every worker was given a quota to be filled without debate; over-fulfillment was routinely demanded. In practice, this meant work harder, eat less. Quantity trumped quality. Misleading trade and industry statistics were enshrined in the Permanent Exhibition of Economic Achievement in Moscow. Erstwhile heroes of the Soviet Union were erased from history books and even from photographs. Terror and coercion became the mainstays of the system.

Teachers often quoted Stalin to their classes. "Leaders come and go," the great man had said, "but the People remain." In reality, the people had to come and go; the leader remained. His dream for the collectivization of agriculture was pursued with utter disregard for the cost in human lives. Those who resisted were deported or shot. A fictional social enemy, the *kulak,* was invented to justify the murders. Famine and the deaths of seven million people were dismissed as western propaganda. The truth was common knowledge, but no one acknowledged it. It was safer to live the lie.

So Galina didn't trust too much to her textbooks. Family history, however, endured, and one story in particular held its own through countless repetitions at the dinner table. Her father choked with laughter every time her mother told it. The incident had occurred when Galina's mother, Nina, was twelve years old.

It was 1917. The war people thought would be over in months had dragged on for three years, with no end in sight. Tsar Nicholas vowed to fight on until the last enemy was driven from Russian soil. But the enemy lingered and the St. Petersburg crowds that had cheered when Europe gaily embarked on its own destruction now gathered in protest. The Guards officers who had packed their dress uniforms for an early victory parade down Unter den Linden lay among the millions already dead and wounded. The Russian army was a colossus: more than fifteen million men were harnessed to the "steamroller," but the crushing impact of massive manpower was shattered by quick-firing artillery and the machine gun. By 1917, the troops who marched under the Imperial double eagle were no longer men gallantly making the supreme sacrifice for their country. They were simply men who were going to die.

At the outset of war, mobs sacked the German embassy in St. Petersburg and the tsar changed the city's name to Petrograd, which sounded more Slavonic. Three years into the slaughter, the people's high morale had turned into a terrible anger. Trainloads of wounded soldiers slid daily into Warsaw Station. Thousands of refugees from Russia's lost territories crammed into wooden sheds and cellars nearby. Many were shoeless, their children still dressed only in the thin cotton clothes of their summer flight. Bread queues stretched for blocks; the windows of bakeries were smashed at night. The poor, who couldn't afford wood for heat, shivered in apartments kept barely above freezing. Speculators flourished, sharks greedily working their financial jaws as the cost of bread quadrupled and the price of aspirin soared a hundredfold. Cabarets and cafes flourished. Prohibition, introduced at the outset of war, crippled government finances, but the rich slipped bootleg vodka into their pineapple juice and drank it from porcelain teacups. The suicide rate tripled.

In the capital, protests gave way to riots in which politics played little part. A journalist asked the crowds what they wanted. "Bread, peace with the Germans, and freedom for the Yids," he was told. There was more than one bloody clash on the streets. Tsar Nicholas surrendered his crown; the government was a shambles. No one doubted that a revolution was underway.

In Nina's home the word was spoken in such veiled tones she suspected 'revolution' meant the sort of wicked woman a nice girl like her would never get to know.

"Naturally, I wanted to see what one looked like, but I could hardly ask my parents," recalled Nina. "So I asked my brother Serge, who claimed to know everything about everything. He'll probably tell you I bullied him into it."

Worn down by his sister's persistence, Serge eventually gave in but, being something of a financial shark himself, he extorted a hefty fee before a date was set for one Sunday after church. When the day came, Nina made sure she had a few coins ready for the collection plate but when the plate was passed, she slipped in only one, holding the others back to pay to her brother. Impatient for the sight of a revolution, she thought the bearded priest would never finish chanting his prayers, or swinging his incense, or intoning his creed. Twice her mother scolded her for fidgeting. Nina got tired of standing. She shifted her weight restlessly from one foot to the other, casting envious glances at the elderly arthritics who occupied the folding chairs along the walls.

At last, the service ended. Nina escaped to the vestibule, where she quickly lost her mother in a crowd of chattering women, each of them dressed as though for a fashion show. Serge was nowhere in sight. He had stopped attending church as soon as he was old enough to choose for himself how to spend his Sunday mornings and Alexander, the Bolshevik, had faith only in the potential of man. Grandfather Peter flatly refused to go. "The only reason *you* go is to show off your new hat," he told his wife. "It's a waste of time." So the men stayed home while Paraskeva paraded three well-dressed daughters and two younger sons down the street to the Greek Church.

Nina never understood why it was called the Greek Church. Some lingering influence from ancient trade routes perhaps, like her mother's name, but no trace of Mediterranean mystery lingered. It was only a plain brown stucco building with a tin roof, where a bearded Orthodox priest dispensed incense and absolution. While her mother's friends assessed each others' clothes in the lobby, Nina eagerly pushed open the heavy wooden door and bounded out onto the steps, anxiously searching the block for her brother.

From across the street, Serge raised a laconic hand in greeting and Nina scurried down the sidewalk, breathless with anticipation at the thought of seeing her first revolution. She caught up with Serge at the corner. Smoothing the ruffles of her dress with one hand, she pulled her money out her pocket with the other. The coins that had not tinkled into the collection plate now slipped soundlessly into Serge's palm.

The early June morning was a harbinger of the bright, warm summer days to come. Throngs of people happily shed the trappings of a too-long winter and strolled the broad avenues of St. Petersburg in a colourful pageant. Nina scanned the faces above the buttons and bows, trying to spot a revolution among the stylish ladies on the Nevsky Prospekt. Young, old, lined cheeks and smooth, she imagined dissipation in all of them, until she was distracted by a shop window full of hats. One in particular caught her eye, a large-brimmed droopy affair in black velvet, topped with a plume of dyed-pink ostrich feathers. Her step slowed as she gazed at the elegant creation. Serge shook her elbow to hurry her along. Nina turned to protest just as gunfire erupted at the end of the block. Pedestrians scattered like leaves in the wind.

"Get down!" Serge yelled.

"I can't!" Nina wailed. "I've got my best white dress on. Mama will kill me if I get it dirty!"

"A bullet will kill you if you don't," Serge replied and roughly pushed her to her knees.

Nina felt a sharp pain as her right shoulder connected heavily with the closed door of the hat shop. She heard the distinctive rip of fine linen as she landed in a heap with Serge crouched protectively over her. From the corner of her eye, she watched

23

an assorted collection of knees, male and female, sweep past as a band of protesters fought to escape the mounted soldiers pursuing them. Banners and placards littered the street as they fled. Bullets whined. One struck the doorway where Serge and Nina huddled, showering bits of concrete on their heads. Nina noticed a splatter of red on her dress. Horrified, she twisted around to look up at her brother and saw blood where a fragment of stone had grazed his cheek. She heard a scream, a shouted order from one of the soldiers, and the thunder of hooves along the pavement. She cowered further into the corner of the doorjamb as a dozen horses, spurred on by their Cossack masters, clattered down the street after the troublemakers.

When the final hoofbeats died away, brother and sister unfolded themselves and climbed slowly to their feet. Nina was shaking. Serge dabbed the blood from his face with his handkerchief, then silently took Nina's hand and led her home.

She never quite forgave him, either for ruining her dress or for misleading her about the revolution. And Serge never gave her money back.

ii

The revolution happened twenty years ago, Galina thought, and here we are still worrying about being killed. She grimaced as her father, another Sergei, fitted a gas mask to her face.

"Here, Galya, it goes on like this," he said.

Galina squirmed out of his grasp, hating the clammy feel of the rubber against her skin. It was one thing for Papa to force soldiers to wear the clumsy device, but not his own daughter!

Sergei had fought for the Reds in the civil war that followed the revolution and he still engaged in war games every summer. He had more than done his duty. Two years' service was the minimum required of all men over twenty. Galina wondered if any of them looked as well in their uniforms as her father did. She delighted especially in the rich scent of Sergei's wide leather belt and bandolier.

Since the revolution, there had been no officer class, everyone was a commander. Except those like Sergei, with an education, who were commanders-in-chief. It was part of his job to teach others to recognize and defend against poisonous gases. From time to time, he brought canisters of the stuff home, which made his wife nervous. More than once she had prodded him back out of bed to check that the seals on the tins were tight and that no gas was escaping to waft around the apartment and kill them as they slept.

To his daughter, Sergei said, "You must learn how to use a mask, Galuchka. It's for your own protection."

Protection, Galina thought. Who needs protection against something invisible that smells like geraniums? But her father's tone brooked no argument and she forced herself to stand still while he adjusted the straps to fit her head. She tried not to panic as her world narrowed to a thin strip of light.

"The nose and mouth piece lets the air you inhale pass through the visor without fogging it up. That way you can still see where you are going."

Where Galina wanted to go was away from loudspeakers that warned of imminent attack and billboards that demanded workers achieve "the Five Year Plan in four!" But whether in school, at the cinema, or standing in line at the shops, there was no escaping the sight of the sallow face with the black moustache and heavy eyebrows. Portraits of Stalin were everywhere.

Galina's nanny, Marusia, all but bowed every time she walked past one. The gesture might have looked elegant if Marusia had been tall and slim, but her round body and bland features lacked the necessary grace. Galina attributed the flaw to the servant girl's peasant background.

In theory, class distinction disappeared after the revolution. Galina knew, however, that her father's trusted position among Party officials gave his family a status that others lacked. Her mother also had a job. One happy result of the social upheaval in Russia was that women were now encouraged to pursue education and employment. Even work as a domestic was a step up the ladder for many who came from collective farms. Marusia was one of them. In her case, the door to a better life led through the government registration office which issued the internal passport she needed to move from the collective into Leningrad, where she was placed with the Ivanov family. Sergei and Nina not only paid her a salary but gave her time off in the evenings to go to school. In a few years, she would be ready to move on to bigger and even better things, such as living in the barracks at a factory.

"What was life like on a collective?" Galina asked. She had seen the small farms near Luga, where the wheat and the vegetables they produced were barely enough to feed the farmers' own families. She could scarcely imagine hundreds of thousands of acres being tilled for the State by people who had once owned the land themselves.

An uncomfortable silence followed the question. Sergei sipped his tea. Nina bit her lip. Marusia fussed with cups and saucers, adjusted the spigot on the samovar, and slid the glass dish of sugar cubes closer to Galina. They were seated around the dining table, speaking in low tones that could not be heard in the hallway, talking of things they would never mention outside the family circle.

"It's like this, Galuchka," her father said, "The Party had no hold on the villages. Its leaders didn't understand the peasants and they thought it was blasphemous for them to want to own their own land and livestock."

Nina interrupted dryly, "What about the dream of a rural Utopia? Lenin used to say that the future lay in vast factory farms."

Sergei nodded. "Yes, where villages are swallowed by agro-towns, and wooden cabins and vegetable plots disappear into apartment blocks and restaurants. The Party thought if it could collectivize the farms, the whole countryside would become State property, and so would the people who live there."

"VKP," Marusia said.

Galina was confused. VKP was the acronym for the All-Union Communist Party.

"The *Vtoroe Krepostnoe Pravo*," Marusia explained, "the Second Serfdom." Her voice was expressionless. "After seventy years of emancipation, the Russian peasant has been returned to serfdom at the point of a gun."

Bewildered, Galina looked from her nanny to her parents. During the revolution, her father explained, the great estates and farms that supplied Russia's cities had been taken over by peasants. In the years that followed, almost all the country's grain was produced and consumed by smallholders. In the aftermath of the civil war, there were hardly any city goods for smallholders to buy and the State price for grain didn't cover the cost of producing it. By the late 1920s, there was little incentive for them to sell. Grain was hoarded or eaten on the farms, and the towns and cities went hungry. The Party set quotas and sent out squads to seize the grain. Peasants continued to hide it or sell it illegally to private traders.

Sergei paused to take another sip of tea and consider how to tell his daughter what had happened next. Marusia forestalled him.

"So you see, the State was forced to take full control of the food supply. It had no other option," she said. "Comrade Stalin began the collectivization of all our agriculture."

The half-truths of Party propaganda, even so glibly recited, could not mitigate the human cost of this strategy. In order for collectivization to succeed, Stalin had to incite class hatred in the villages, where peasants were duly categorized as poor, middle,

ANNE METIKOSH · *Chance*

or *kulak*. The word *kulak* meant "fist." Before the revolution, it had been tagged to village moneylenders. Though *kulak* now, in theory, identified a peasant rich enough to hire the labour of others, the name quickly became a catchall. Where a peasant was clearly too beggared for it to apply, he could easily be dealt with as a *podkulachnik,* a *kulak* sympathizer. In Stalin's new revolution, all the country's grain-producing areas were to be collectivized and all *kulaks* liquidated.

"Liquidated?" said Galina.

"Killed."

Galina stared wide-eyed at Marusia. "How did you escape?" she asked.

Marusia looked at the eager child in front of her. At her age, she thought, life was a great adventure for me too. Give this one time. She'll learn the difference between a thrilling exploit and grim reality.

Aloud she said, "I nearly didn't. I was almost taken by the State body collectors." Galina's eyes got even bigger. "This was, you understand, a difficult time. There was no food. People were eating rats, and ants, and earthworms."

"*Eeuw,*" said Galina, screwing up her mouth.

"Many people died. And every so often, the body collectors came. One day, three men, all dressed in black, came to our house. One of them watched the horses, two piled corpses on the cart. They threw on my mother. They threw on my father. He wasn't dead yet, just too weak to protest. He gestured me to go and hide. I hid in my mother's trunk. The men swore and stomped around, but they didn't find me."

"Go on," Galina urged.

Marusia glanced at her employers. Sergei was watching Galina's face closely while Nina braided the fringe on the tablecloth, her lips tightly compressed, her eyes bright with tears.

Marusia took a deep breath. "The corpses were piled up on

the cart like heaps of straw. The body collectors wheeled them to the pit outside the village and tipped them in. They didn't bother to check whether everyone was dead."

The girl waited until the body collectors were gone and then made her way to the train station. In the village square, she passed a naked man covered in dust, fighting with cats over a dead pigeon. The train that took her to the district centre rattled past unharvested fields of corn and wheat. Across the expanse, armed guards in high towers watched for "snippers," people driven by hunger to cut off ears of corn with scissors. Snippers who were caught were sentenced to a minimum of ten years hard labour for stealing State property; some were shot. A doctor who complained that his sister had died of hunger was sentenced to ten years "without the right of correspondence," the euphemism for a death sentence.

Pravda published an article under Stalin's name about the progress of his revolution. The headline read: "Dizzy with success."

A few days later, there was a light tap at the door. Galina wasn't even sure she had heard anything. She felt a shiver of fear run down her back when her mother went to the door and opened it a crack. It couldn't be anyone they knew; a friend would have knocked properly. Galina abandoned her homework on the dining room table and tiptoed up behind her mother, peering past her shoulder at the woman standing in the hall.

It was hard to judge the woman's age. Her skin had a yellow cast to it, and her head nodded awkwardly on a neck that looked too frail to support it. Arms thin as matchsticks were held out in mute supplication from sleeves too short to cover them. Her patched grey overcoat could not hide the distended belly underneath. Galina was shocked to see that apart from the coat, the woman was naked.

"Please," the woman whispered, "please." Her palms were calloused and there was dirt caked under her broken fingernails.

Nina didn't ask the woman in but, leaving the door ajar, quickly wrapped a half loaf of bread and two roubles in a towel and handed them to her. There was nothing else to give her: Marusia hadn't returned with the day's groceries.

iii

Galina and her nanny stood in a queue. Marusia spent part of every day standing in line to buy things. Galina was glad she only had to join her when there wasn't any school. It was boring waiting in line; the conversation with strangers was always the same. "What are they giving today?" people asked. And always on a note of false optimism, because the answer didn't really matter. Whatever was being sold was what they would eat for dinner. There was no point saying "Wouldn't corn be nice" when there was only cabbage to be had.

But today they hoped to buy shoes, and so did the hundreds of others who had been joining the queue since daybreak. People were beginning to get restless. Any minute now the police would appear to break up the crowd. A ripple of apprehension ran down the line as the customers numbered off and prepared to scatter. Not two minutes later, there was a clatter of hooves on the pavement. Four mounted officers rode straight at the lineup, ordering the crowd to disperse.

Marusia gripped Galina's hand and hustled her away.

"We'll take a little walk," she said, "and come back when the police are gone. We're number thirty-six, so we shouldn't have to wait too long next time."

They slipped down a side street, peeking in the windows of the dentist and the dressmaker and the Armenian shoemaker. At this last window, Galina's step slowed. A single pair of shoes was on display. Red strapped shoes with white kid leather inside, the kind of shoes Galina had only dreamed of. She stopped and stared. She was used to getting a new pair of shoes every year or two. They all looked the same, black boots with low heels that came up past her ankles, the laces tied through a myriad of eyelets. Some years they were relatively sturdy and, with repair, lasted until a new pair could be bought. With others, as now, shoddy workmanship showed in the flaps of sole that caught on the pavement and tripped her up on the stairs. Never had she owned a pair of shoes like the ones in the window. The Armenian must be one of the private businesses the Soviets allowed for an extra fee; the taxes they paid were more than included in the prices they charged. Only the lucky ones with enough hard currency were entitled to buy.

"Those," Galina sighed. "Those are the shoes I want."

"Don't be ridiculous," snapped Marusia. "It would cost your mother two months' salary to buy shoes like that. Even your parents aren't that indulgent."

They wandered beneath the towering maple trees in the Alexandrov Gardens, past the statues of Gogol and Glinka, and on to the fountain in front of the Admiralty building. Galina waved her hands through the jets of water encircling the pool and laughed as rainbows scattered across it. Beyond the fountain she could see the Neva River and opposite where she stood, the eastern tip of Vasilevsky Island, where she lived.

"We'd better go back for the shoes," Marusia said. They crossed the square where the bronze statue of Peter the Great on his horse stood poised to leap the river. To the east was the Winter Palace. From here the city fanned out to the south along three broad avenues, one of which led to the station where Galina and her grandmother caught the train to Luga every summer.

iv

Galina studied the face of Tsar Nicholas pictured in the magazine open in front of her. She was seated in a hard-backed chair at Businka's dining table. Her brow wrinkled with concentration as she copied the picture onto a blank sheet of paper. She felt like a true artist as she washed colour onto it, nodding her head in satisfaction at the result. She considered the original image in the magazine again and decided it lacked something. Grinning, she touched the tip of her paintbrush to the tsar's lips, staining them red. She wondered if his children had ever made drawings of him and if he had laughed at them, or if he had been too busy with matters of state to care. A postcard of the imperial family stood in a small gilt easel on a bookshelf in the apartment. It was a souvenir to celebrate the 300-year anniversary of Romanov rule. In it, the tsar and tsarina stared straight ahead, their expressions matching those of their five children. The tsarevitch, Alexei, was dressed in a sailor suit. His mother and sisters wore gauzy white dresses. All of them had the confident look of people whose future is secure.

Galina wondered what had really happened to them. There were so many rumours. Some said they had all fled Russia for England; some said they had all been killed. The romantic suggested the parents were dead but one of the daughters had escaped. Galina imagined a handsome young soldier and a daring rescue. It must have been wonderful, she thought, to be the daughter of a tsar.

Her own father was something of a fairy tale figure in her life because he was frequently absent from it. Though from time to time his temper flared, when he was in good humour he treated her like a princess. She often relived the memory of that wonderful day in November when he had taken her to see her first ballet.

The hall was gold, the seats covered in blue velvet, and crystal chandeliers hung from the ceiling. Outside, sunshine streamed across the square, but no daylight penetrated the world of fantasy within. Every seat in the theatre was taken and in the gallery people stood, craning forward to see past one another's shoulders. Whispered comments and the crackling of programs filled the air. In the front row of the first balcony, a little girl with a crown of braided hair leaned over the polished brass rail, taut with excitement as she waited for Act Two to begin. Beside her, her father studied the program as though nothing else mattered in the world but the fact that on this afternoon in September, Tchaikovsky's *Snow Maiden* would be danced at the Mariinsky Theatre and he had brought his daughter Galina to see it.

Sergei Nikolayevich Ivanov was a cultured, educated, charming man. Of average height and slight build, he wore his sideburns long and full, perhaps to compensate for the thinning on top that he hid under a cloth cap. He was a dutiful son, an ardent husband, a devoted father, a man who took no interest in the ideological struggles that had sent so many of his countrymen to the gulag. People said he had been born with his tongue hanging in the right direction. He turned this talent to his advantage within a political system he despised.

His father, Nikolai, had been an optician and Sergei was schooled to take over his father's business. When revolution intervened, Nikolai disappeared, his business was confiscated, and Sergei was conscripted to fight for the Communists in the civil war. When the Reds claimed victory, he was discharged to fill the role the Party assigned: work in a glass factory, where his education gave him an advantage over most of his fellow workers and many of the Party leaders as well. The Party now controlled a country of 170 million people, the vast majority of them illiterate and impoverished. Sergei's bosses increasingly relied on him to write their speeches and handle their correspondence.

His wife warned him to tread carefully. Balancing on the fine line of Party approval was a dangerous exercise. "The higher you climb," Nina admonished, "the harder you'll fall." Sergei laughed, but when he was invited to join the Party, he declined, declaring himself unworthy of the honour.

In the theatre, the chandeliers dimmed and the audience grew still. The conductor raised his baton and the woodland tones of an oboe drifted up to the balcony. The heavy stage curtain opened. Lights played across a wintry backdrop and settled on the vaulted doorway of an icehouse, where a ballerina appeared. This was the snow maiden. She twirled to the soaring music. The sequins of her costume dazzled.

Galina wished her mother could have been there, but tickets to the ballet were hard to get. Companies obtained them in bulk to use as employee incentives. Sergei was given two. He had planned to escort his wife but his daughter's persistent pleas changed his mind.

All the way home, Galina walked on tiptoe in her high boots, admiring her reflection in every window. She couldn't wait to see herself en pointe in the full-length mirror at home.

"I'm going to be a ballerina, Papa."

Sergei smiled. "Whatever you like, Galuchka. But for now, be careful where you step!" He reached out a hand to stop her twirling over the curb and into the path of a passing *droshky*. "We don't want you melting away from us like the Snow Maiden."

Galina slipped her hand through her father's arm, just as her mother did, and suffered the usual disenchantment as they left behind the glittering facades of the theatre. She ignored the drab uniformity of the people in the street, imagining instead the fading palaces along the *prospekt* still brilliant with throngs of guests in dazzling silk gowns and gold braid. Long evening shadows aided her fancy, changing the shape of streets and buildings from the familiar to the fantastic.

Her dancing steps slowed as they neared home.

The Ivanovs occupied the apartment allotted to them by the government. They had private living quarters but shared a kitchen and a bath with two other families assigned by the local soviet. The state had determined that each of its citizens was entitled to six square metres of space. But that didn't mean that a little extra cash or a glib tongue couldn't buy you more, and smooth-talking Sergei had used his talent to obtain a small additional room for his family.

The building the Ivanovs lived in was one of the square concrete blocks that had sprouted like mushrooms during the Communist building spree of the 1920s. They were hastily and poorly built, uniformly dull in comparison to the fairy tale splendours of the baroque palaces that lined the embankment. By the time the first tenants moved in, the painted wooden floors were already scuffed and the grey walls dingy.

Galina and her father climbed dimly lit stairs to the second floor. Their shoes left footprints in the dust. A musty odour drifted up from the basement. Leningrad was a city to rival Venice for its interplay of water and stone, granite piles, and slender bridges. It had been built on the Neva marshes at the cost of uncounted lives, its royal residences and public buildings designed by the most gifted architects. But even the most beautiful structure, if set below the water line, floods with the regularity of the tide.

The second-floor landing opened into a hall painted the same flat colour as the stairwell. The Ivanovs lived in the room at the end of the corridor, but Galina first detoured into the kitchen to wash her hands. Only there did the unforgiving grey décor give way, though the difference was negligible; the kitchen walls were painted cream to midpoint and olive to the floor.

Vera Michailovna was in the kitchen preparing the evening meal for herself and her aged mother. She was an angular woman with curiously immobile features and unsmiling eyes. Her husband had died during an investigation, after the production quotas for his factory went unmet. Shortly afterward, her son Yuri had been invited to join one of the work battalions constructing the Volga-Don canal. It was a standing joke that anyone unlucky enough to work on the project would be *dolgavon,* a long time away, but Galina didn't think Vera Michailovna would appreciate the play on words.

"That smells good," Galina said, nodding toward a bubbling pot of soup.

"Always more of the same," Vera Michailovna said, directing her morose commentary to the ladle in her hand. She abandoned her cabbage and carrots long enough to retrieve a small saucepan from the cupboard below the tabletop primus.

Galina eyed the other two tables in the room. The Chulitsky's was littered with the remains of their supper. On the west wall, the Ivanov's table showed no sign of a meal in progress. Galina sighed. The ice cream Papa had treated her to had only whetted her appetite. Her stomach was beginning to grumble.

Galina turned on the faucet and rinsed her hands, wincing a little under the cold spray. All new buildings in Leningrad were equipped with central heating, as the Communists prided themselves on their advanced technology, but only the cold water actually worked.

Glancing out the window to the courtyard below, Galina counted half a dozen children playing there. The two smallest squatted in the sandbox, solemnly filling buckets and upending them, as they built a fortress to rival the Peter and Paul. Galina wondered whose mother was watching them. At that age, children sat in the dirt without thought. Only the repeated scold about germs made sitting on your heels automatic.

Vera Michailovna's dialogue with her soup pot was drowned by a sudden rattle and gush. Involuntarily, Galina's eye went to the high narrow window that opened into the kitchen from the toilet. It was too bad, Galina thought, that the only source of fresh air was from kitchen to courtyard. Mr. Chulitsky emerged from the toilet pulling his suspenders back up over his shoulders. Galina fled down the hall to her family's quarters.

Mama and Tante Lily had their heads together over a magazine. Cigarette smoke hung like a wreath over Mama's braid and Tante's pin curls. Papa's face was hidden behind a newspaper, but a telltale cloud drifted out around its edges. Galina smiled, remembering the abortive attempt both her parents had made to quit smoking. Each had solemnly declared an end to the filthy habit, formally shaking hands to seal the bargain. There would be no more nicotine stains on their fingers, no more lingering smell or telltale burns on their clothing, no more stale, clotted air in the apartment. They began in earnest, but ended with each of them hiding an emergency ration of cigarettes behind the same mirror and collapsing into laughter when they discovered each other's perfidy. Since then, they had resigned themselves to their weakness.

Galina had tried smoking once. When Uncle Serge was in town, he stayed at his mother's apartment. Her apartment was built in the days of Peter the Great, when indoor plumbing was unheard of. Two hundred years later, with windowed rooms at a premium, bathrooms had been added wherever there was an empty alcove. They were vented into a hallway. That's where the trouble began.

Uncle Serge liked to stockpile his smokes. He rolled his own two dozen or more at a time and stored them in a carved wooden box on the desk. Galina decided to pilfer one. All the grownups she knew and admired smoked. Mama looked particularly elegant with a cigarette in an amber holder lightly resting between her fingers. While she and Uncle Serge were sharing tea and conversation with their mother, Galina quietly moved to the desk, lifted the lid of the box, and tucked a cigarette up her sleeve. No one paid any attention when she left the room, mumbling that she needed to use the toilet.

She scurried down the hall and locked herself in. From her sleeve she extracted the purloined cigarette, from the pocket of her dress, a box of matches she had lifted from the stovetop in the kitchen. Lacking a holder, she stuck the cigarette directly between her lips, trying to like the taste. She was lucky with the matches. The very first one caught and flared and Galina touched it to the end of the cigarette, pleased at how quickly the scratchy paper and pungent tobacco took the flame. Smoke curled upward, making her eyes tear, but she kept the cigarette firmly clamped in her mouth as she shook out the match and looked for somewhere to put it. A thousand times her mother and grandmother had told her never to throw anything into the toilet, so she didn't even consider that. The only other thing in the room was a basket that held the small squares of old newsprint used as wipes. Sometimes Galina wished she were still two years old. Mothers used a light, washable towel on very young children, but as soon as they were old enough to clean themselves, they graduated to the coarser, but disposable, paper. With no other option in view, Galina tossed her spent match into the basket.

For a minute or two she concentrated very hard on trying to smoke the cigarette. The end seemed to be burning all right, but surely the stinging sensation in nose and throat meant she was doing something wrong? So far, she couldn't see what pleasure people took from smoking. Suddenly she realized she couldn't see, period. Smoke filled the little room, eddying up the walls and out the narrow opening near the ceiling. Galina glanced wildly from the cigarette in her hand to the basket of toilet paper, all but invisible now under a dense grey cloud.

Before she could even think about what to do, there was a commotion in the hallway and Uncle Serge shouldered the door open and burst in to throw a pot of water on the smouldering pile of paper.

Her family never let her forget how she'd nearly incinerated them all, but the episode had quashed any further inclination to smoke.

Papa had retired to his chair, oblivious to the ladies' remarks about the latest Finnish or French fashions. Mama and Tante Lily looked up, smiling, when Galina came into the room, welcoming her into the feminine circle. Galina adored discussions about clothes, and smuggled western magazines, passed surreptitiously from friend to friend, were an endless source of fascination. Her aunt slavishly copied European fads; her mother, though more conservative, had a natural eye for style. New cloth was scarce, but the sisters still had access to their mother's prerevolutionary wardrobe. In those days, the family had considered only the finest material acceptable, so dated garments that had worn well could easily be recut to a more modern look. There was nothing dated about Tante Lily's look, Galina thought admiringly. She adopted even the most impractical styles if a magazine photo tempted her and she always drew attention in the street with her daringly short skirts. While a Leningrad winter found most people covered to the eyebrows, Lily would abandon both muff and muffler to show off the cut of her coat and the elegance of her thin leather gloves.

Galina considered the two women in front of her. Tante, she thought, was definitely chic, but Mama had elegance.

γ

When Galina's mother fell in love, her parents didn't approve. The Ustinovich family descended from nobility. Nina's father

was a banker to counts and grand dukes and had been decorated by the tsar; her mother had friends at court. By contrast, the Ivanovs were mere tradespeople. Although Nina had
eventually won their consent, Peter and Paraskeva continued
to hold their son-in-law at arm's length. They demanded as part
of the marriage agreement that their daughter retain a double
name, Ivanova-Ustinovich, so as not to lose the cachet of her
ancestry.

In the early days of their marriage, the young couple had
lived in Luga, which suited Nina just fine. Away from the city, the
Communist influence was less keenly felt. Prying eyes were less
likely to notice if one wandered into a church to light a candle,
and wagging tongues were less inclined to repeat incautious
remarks. The safest course in the new Russia was to keep one's
head down and mouth shut. But Sergei was as ambitious as he
was self-confident. Opportunity lay with the Party officials and
they didn't live in Luga.

They didn't live in St. Petersburg anymore either, though its
citizens still fondly called it "Peter." It had briefly been called
Petrograd and was now officially Leningrad. For Tsar Nicholas
and his family, this city had been the capital of the world and the
seat of their absolute authority. For Lenin, it was the ideal place
for agitation, intrigue, and revolution. By whatever name and
for whatever purpose, it was never anything but magnificent.
There were those who found it oppressive and tragic. To others
it seemed ethereal and magical. But always it evoked superla-
tives with the majesty of its spaces, the richness of its planes,
the lowering skies of its winter, and the long white nights of its
summer. Here Pavlov trained his dogs, Mendeleyev discovered
the periodic table, Mussorgsky wrote his wild, dark music, and
Pushkin his soaring poetry. Here Pavlova danced her way into
the hearts of the people and the Imperial Ballet showcased the
genius of Diaghilev and Nijinsky. St. Petersburg was Russia's

workshop, its laboratory, the cradle of its scholarship and art, the capital of its creative life.

In 1918, under imminent threat from the German army, Lenin "temporarily" moved the seat of Russian government from St. Petersburg to Moscow. Twenty years later, it was still there. And with Moscow in charge, the people's revolution became more heavy-handed. The residents of Peter had reason to fear the change.

Moscow was wary of St. Petersburg, the city with its heart on the Volga, but its eyes on the brilliance of Paris and Rome. St. Petersburg was progressive, stylish, and, in the mind of the country's new leader, dangerous. Josef Stalin wielded power like a dull sabre, spreading a gruesome trail of blood across the land as he hacked away at his adversaries. And nowhere did his Terror strike more harshly than in Peter.

In the early summer of 1937, while ten-year-old Galina sat dreaming under the trees at her grandmother's dacha, her father was working at a hydroelectric station just east of the city. Sergei had his own office there: a cubicle large enough for a desk, a chair, and a small filing cabinet, with walls painted the same disheartening grey as the ones in his apartment.

He looked up when a knock came at the door and his mouth went dry at the sight of two NKVD officers. They flashed their purple identity cards. Involuntarily, Sergei glanced at his watch. It was four in the afternoon. The NKVD usually made their calls between eleven at night and three in the morning, when the fear factor was greatest and those still half asleep had to grope clumsily for their clothes before they were hustled out the door. Everyone in Russia kept a small bag packed, ready for the knock that came in the night. No one slept well. They had become a country of insomniacs.

"Sergei Nikolayevich Ivanov?"

"Yes."

"You will come with us."

Like everyone else, Sergei had heard the well-worn joke about the arrest squad knocking on a door. "You've made a mistake," says the man who answers it. "The Communists live upstairs."

The joke seemed pointless now.

There was no time to make a phone call, no time to gather up photos or clean clothes. Sergei was frog-marched out of the plant. The silent menace of the NKVD stifled any protest from colleagues who averted their eyes as he passed, unwilling to be involved in someone else's disaster. Outside, one of the black sedans known as Ravens waited.

Nina was never officially notified of her husband's arrest. Not until days later did she learn the news, and then only from the cleaning woman at the power station, who had sneaked into the city to tell her. Nina understood what it meant. In order to protect herself and her child, she would be forced to denounce her husband, renounce his name, and divorce him. When school resumed in the fall, there would be forms to fill out for Galina and the awful truth would have to become public. Meanwhile, Nina did not even know where Sergei was being held. Nor could she find out without exposing herself to danger.

It was her mother-in-law, Anna, who for weeks haunted the offices of the NKVD, the city jails, and the bathhouses that had been pressed into use as prisons, searching for clues to her son's whereabouts, until piece by dreadful piece the story came together.

Nina's younger sister, Tatiana, had married an architect named Ivan. One of his projects was the design of a bridge in Moscow. Unfortunately, the bridge collapsed. In Stalinist Russia, the only acceptable explanation for such a disaster was sabotage and Ivan was duly arrested.

Denunciation was the engine that drove the purges of the 1930s. A vast network of secret informers haunted every workplace and every neighbourhood. They had either to unmask traitors or themselves stand accused. Among the victims of this system were a seventy-year-old schoolteacher guilty of using a textbook that still had a picture of Trotsky in it, a man who took down a portrait of Stalin while painting a wall, a woman who made the sign of the cross when a funeral procession passed by, and a philatelist whose stamp of Queen Victoria had a higher face value than one of Stalin.

In cases of sabotage, an offender might be offered a lighter sentence in exchange for naming ten fellow plotters, real or imagined. Among the ten names that Ivan brought forward was Sergei's.

Sergei didn't know that his own brother-in-law had branded him a saboteur, but it hardly mattered. Once accused, always convicted.

For weeks he languished in prison, a place where denunciation of one's fellows carried even more weight than it did on the street. The first question an interrogator asked was always: "Who recruited you?" The second was: "And whom did you recruit?" Beatings, sleep deprivation, and solitary confinement all encouraged prisoners to name names.

When it finally came, Sergei's trial as an enemy of the state lasted a mere fifteen minutes. Only the famous had their confessions orchestrated: show trials masked the true nature and scale of the main operations. People like Sergei simply disappeared.

"Sergei Ivanov, you are charged in the matter of the Gorkii Bridge which was built by the wishes and to the glory of our benevolent leader Josef Stalin," the court declared. "It collapsed. Sabotage is indicated."

Sergei considered that inferior materials and poorly maintained machinery were more likely indicated, but he kept these traitorous thoughts to himself. In Soviet Russia, perfection was the official standard in all things. According to the Party, just as citizens were uniformly well fed and happy, engineering and building materials were always of the highest calibre. To suggest otherwise was treason.

As he shuffled into the prosecutor's office in chains, Sergei recognized an old schoolmate among the jurors. Viktor Petrovich avoided eye contact. He listened in silence to the "evidence" that damned his old friend as a saboteur.

The Soviets employed three main instruments of terror: the NKVD, a dependent judiciary, and a vast network of concentration camps. By 1937, these had expanded to the point where the manpower of the security agencies rivalled that of the Red Army, and the camps contained nearly ten percent of the population. By 1939, the Gulag was the largest employer in Europe. Its employees, the *zeks,* were systematically starved and overworked in arctic conditions: their average life expectancy was one winter. Victims were rounded up singly and en masse and charged with sabotage, treason, or espionage, then tortured, executed, or sentenced to fixed periods of imprisonment from which very few emerged alive. Since every victim was expected to denounce ten or twenty accomplices and their families, it was only a matter of time before the numbers involved were counted in the thousands, and in the end, the millions.

When the guard left the room for a moment, Viktor Petrovich leaned toward Sergei, his face expressionless, his lips barely moving. "I'm sorry," he whispered in Sergei's ear. "I can't do much for you my friend. The best we can hope for is one of the better camps." There was no question of serving less time. Ten years hard labour was the automatic sentence for saboteurs.

Sergei was shipped to Siberia.

When he managed, months later, to smuggle out a letter, he sent it not to his wife but to his mother. Any direct communication would have compromised Nina's safety, and Galina's. So it was Anna who told them that he had broken his leg working in a lumber camp, that he was in the hospital there, that he was recovering. Anna was desperate to see him but, even as she packed for Siberia, Sergei was transferred to Karaganda, on the endless desert steppe of Kazakhstan. His mother revised her plans. A long trip to the other end of the country yielded one brief visit. She brought back a single photo of Sergei, dated 1939. It was the last anyone heard of him.

Soon after Anna's return, the bust of Lenin, which had held such pride of place in her living room, disappeared.

Anna's Lament

In the beyond, she saw her son
His eyes upturned like stone

"Let go of me, Mother! Let go!
The thunderstorm has swept me forever into its net"

...Nothing left for me now but building a rosary
from relics of his face
With calloused hands
I tend the hardened plants of Memory
A time to pluck, a time to plant again...

Lest I forget in the whirlwind of death
the rattle of Black Ravens or
the pounding on the door or
the women howling like wounded beasts at bay...

Seventeen moons I've howled by the gates,
wooing the hangman with my mating call...
Come home my son!

vi

When Galina returned from Luga at the end of the summer, her mother seemed much older than when she had left. Or maybe it was simply the greyness of the city that had drained the colour from her cheeks. The engine was still hissing when the conductor held out his hand to help Galina from the train. Businka close behind her, the girl searched the crowd for her mother and in a moment, spotted her and waved. Nina trembled as she wrapped her arms around her daughter.

"Galina," she said, "Galya ... little one ..."

The bad news was there, in the hesitation in Nina's voice and her inability to settle on a name. Galina recoiled from the pain in her mother's face, feeling herself spiral inward. She had never thought of her parents objectively, as people, any more than she had her aunts, uncles, cousins, or grandparents. All of them simply existed, unquestioned, in their relationships to her. When she learned her father was gone, she hugged herself tightly and somewhere inside felt a tiny thud, like the muffled closing of a door.

It would have been easier, she thought, if Papa had been killed outright. That way, there would have been a body to bury and a grave to weep over. As it was, her sense of loss was soon over-shadowed by a sense of dread, and although some of her anxiety was for her father, more of it was for herself. What might happen to her as a result of what had happened to him? Papa was lost: there was nothing to be done about it. But she and Mama would now join the ranks of those who lost sleep over the sound of Black Ravens in the street and who shrank from the knock on the door. As a result of her father's arrest, their names would now be on The List. Like everyone in Leningrad, Galina knew how easily one person's offence could be extended to others, and with how little provocation the NKVD could step in and make an arrest. The mild paranoia of life in the Soviet Union had now deepened into all out Terror.

In the early 1930s, while Stalin embarked on the first of his five-year plans in Moscow, Leningrad produced her own brilliant leader. Sergei Kirov steadily won over members of the Central Committee until, in December 1934, he was assassinated. Rumour, quickly stifled, hinted that Stalin himself had masterminded the plot. Whatever the truth, Kirov's murder gave the man of steel all the excuse he needed to launch a witchhunt that bloodied Russia from one end to the other. Everyone knew at least one among the thousands, now growing to millions, arrested and shot or sent to concentration camps. The long-dreaded secret police had been handed the power to sentence and execute anyone in the country. Their targets were any who suggested a lack of sympathy for the regime, even schoolchildren.

In honour of the Kirov assassination, a factory, a ballet company, and several towns were renamed and a school holiday was proclaimed. The children were delighted. Galina's friend Nadia danced around the classroom.

"Just think," she said. "If Comrade Stalin were assassinated, we might have a two-day holiday!"

The next morning, Nadia's parents were arrested and the state took over care of their orphan.

Galina dreaded the thought of going back to school. How would she cope with the pointing fingers, the whispered comments, the open stares? It was one thing for her mother to publicly repudiate her father — that was necessary window dressing. But Nina was quietly burning his letters and diaries too. Was any of it incriminating? How could they know? Once official doubt had attached to your name, even the most innocuous note could be made suspicious. A sentimental attachment to love letters was not worth the risk of a trip to the gulag. It wouldn't bring Sergei back, and it would make Galina an orphan.

When Galina looked at her mother, she saw a window with the

shades pulled down. There was something gone from Nina's face that the child remembered there. She checked her own image in the mirror before she left the apartment, seeking reassurance from the even features and the thick braid beneath the rakish black beret. Galina noticed that her mouth looked tight and her eyes glittered on the verge of tears. In spite of holding herself rigid and taking three deep breaths as she always did when she was nervous, her fingers trembled when she handed her teacher the registration paper that detailed her parent's occupations. Beside her mother's name was neatly printed "bookkeeper." Fine. Nina had a good job in a respectable government office. But beside her father's name, the words "exiled, enemy of the state" leap from the page like demons. Head bowed, she waited for the public denunciation that must surely follow. None came.

Relieved and more than a little surprised, Galina took her seat, glancing covertly at the faces of her classmates as she straightened her books on the desk in front of her.

"Did you hear?" Irina whispered.

"What?"

"Katya's father. Mother too."

"And my uncle."

"My brother."

Half a dozen at least, in my classroom alone, Galina thought. I am not the only one.

Members of the group quickly learned to adopt the latest in defensive weapons: the unmoving countenance. Admiration and contempt, love and hate were still active behind their polite social masks but the children, who were still mastering their math tables, had learned that it was imprudent to show them.

Nina worried she might lose her job. The same information that Galina presented at school was also required at Nina's workplace. If he were so inclined, her boss would be within his rights to fire her: since her husband was obviously disloyal to the state, in all likelihood, so was she. Nina's stomach tightened as she handed Igor Mironov the damning missive. He deliberated, fingering the greying beard he had adopted the same year he had abandoned the name Himmelfarb. Before 1917, only a small number of Jews had been allowed to live in St. Petersburg. It was common in tsarist Russia to change one's name to something less semitic sounding, or to subtly alter one's appearance in order to advance. Many of the leaders of the revolution had followed the trend: they were born with names like Bronstein and Apfelbaum but their followers knew them as Trotsky and Zinoviev.

Once the Bolsheviks were in power, the Jews became a favoured minority, hired and promoted on a quota system designed to redress the old social imbalance. One of the first laws enacted in the new state made anti-semitism a crime. Exactly what that meant was rather nebulous, but it wasn't a test many wanted to meet.

Hurrying to work one day through the crush on the Nevsky *prospekt*, Nina bumped into a matronly woman, knocking her slightly off balance. Nina stopped to apologize. But the woman rounded on her and loudly accused her, not of rudeness or clumsiness, but of being an anti-semite — an offence now punishable by arrest. Forgetting the apology, Nina fled.

Igor Mironov was a sympathetic man. He glanced up at Nina and nodded. There was no expression on his face as he stuffed the cursed paper under a pile of others on his desk. With luck it would never surface.

Luck was something they were all going to need. Russia had signed a nonaggression pact with Germany, and she stood on the sidelines while Hitler crushed Poland and France, then turned his sights on Britain. But it wouldn't be long before the Fuhrer reneged and loosed his hordes on the Soviet Union.

Galina, and millions like her, were about to become pawns in a monstrous game of chance.

PARADISE LOST

Yugoslavia, 1941

❧

The idyll on Lokrum lasted until Dragan was eleven, when even Uncle Dragutin's influence could not extend it. Most special case students were only allowed to stay on the island for one year, two at most. Dragan, Milica, and Maria had been there for three. It was time to go home. But not to Bijele Vode. That part of life was over.

While he was at Lokrum, Gligo and Mileva had moved from the village to the town of Petrinja, a move which signalled a small step up in their fortunes. Their new home nestled in the foothills on a wide plain by the river Petrinchica, a tributary of the Sava. Their farmyard now boasted ten cows, two horses, and an assortment of pigs, chickens and geese. It fell to Dragan to milk the cows. Every day he delivered fresh pails of frothy liquid to the neighbours on his way to school and picked up the empty cans on the way home. Though the family was better off than it had been in Bijele Vode, survival still meant there was no time for idleness. Spring, summer, or fall, there were always crops to be planted, cultivated, or harvested; fruit to be preserved or turned into brandy; animals to be bred, fattened, and slaughtered; wool and flax to be spun and woven into cloth. All the family had, they made with their own hands.

Winter provided some respite from their labours, when a dazzling sun turned the undulating plains and snow-laden pines

50

into an impossibly lovely Christmas card. With the snow lying thick on sleeping fields, Dragan had the leisure to knock staves out of an old barrel and fashion them into skis. Clambering up a hill, he paused at the top only long enough to tie the skis onto his boots with a piece of wire, before pushing himself off for the long glide down through glistening powder.

Summer months were the busiest. The men worked long hours under a punishing sun, scything down fields of golden grain that waved gently into the blurred purple distance, while their wives hoed the straight lines of vegetables that grew in their yards. Boys like Dragan led the cows and horses to the river to sluice dust and sweat from the animals' backs. Ripening plums glowed like amethysts on the trees and the scent of honeysuckle and new-mown hay drifted in the evening air.

Any gathering of crops was an excuse for a gathering of neighbours. When it was time to harvest the wheat, they brought their scythes; for oats, barley, and rye, their sickles. The *zetva* was a social event and the end of a hard day's work was celebrated with plenty of food, music, and dancing. Dragan's favourite celebrations were the *berbas*, the fruit harvests. He loved climbing barefoot into vast wooden barrels to stomp sliced plums or pearly grapes into the juice that would ferment into *rakija* or wine.

In the years before government intervention, when the private production of liquor was still the norm, Gligo Metikos had the biggest and the best vineyard in the region. It provided extra income for the family and insured that Gligo always had plenty of friends around. When it was time to fill the barrels, neighbourhood men went from vineyard to vineyard to help distill, pour, and cap. They remained long into the night sampling each other's wares. No one looked askance when they finally stumbled home, roaring drunk, to beat their wives and throw their sons out into the streets.

By March of 1941, Dragan had almost made it through the five-year slog of teacher's college. Sitting at his desk in the half-empty classroom, he tried to concentrate on the wording of his essay and ignore the hubbub in the courtyard, where student leaders were setting up for another political rally. Two more months, Dragan thought, and he would be looking for a job in Zagreb, or maybe even Belgrade. He had yearned to study agronomy, but there had been no scholarship spots available at the university, and he had no money for tuition. Teaching was his second choice. It was an honourable profession by any standard and even though it would take him away from the farm, for a boy whose main talent was a good memory, it was a tolerable option.

Dragan enjoyed college. He was used to hard work and he was proud of the inked indicators of success that marked his steady progress. The diploma he sought would transform the dreams he held for the future into reality.

Many of his friends were dreamers too; in a country still closely tied to the land, the heaven-on-earth Eden painted by the Progressive Students' Union at the college was bound to attract them. The campus agitators who promoted the Communist doctrine appealed to the students' idealistic vision of the world and dismissed reports of the shortcomings of the Soviet system as western propaganda. The Russian door to the west had slammed firmly shut after Josef Stalin took power. When rumours of famine in the Ukraine, slave labour on the Volga, and the exile of thousands to Murmansk filtered through the cracks, they were given short shrift. Truth lived in the printed pamphlets the Union leaders handed out and in the speeches they so ardently addressed to the eager crowds on campus. Russia, the students believed, was a great nation doing great things. If fulfillment of the Communist dream meant the arrest of two or three million enemies of the state, so be it. It was a small price to pay, especially in a country of 200 million people.

As the clock ticked over to the hour, a ruler banged down on the top of a wooden desk. Twenty young men and women jumped, then bent their heads and scribbled feverishly to finish sentences and best guess answers.

"Time's up," said the grey-haired autocrat at the front of the room.

The students groaned and exchanged frustrated looks before bowing to the inevitable and abandoning their pens to shuffle together *Practical Teaching Techniques,* Gorki's novel *Mother,* and copies of a newspaper called *The Students' Voice.* Dragan traded smiles with a pretty classmate named Dara, but before he could speak to her, his friend Marko clapped him on the shoulder.

"So, Dragan, have you made up your mind yet?" Marko fingered the beard he trimmed so carefully to match Lenin's. "It'd be a snap to get you a membership in the Party."

"Well, you know, I'm still thinking about it."

"What's to think about? The evidence is clear. Read the newspapers. Collectivisation is working like a charm in Russia. The Communists have created the perfect society there."

Dragan tapped the copy of *The Students' Voice* that Marko carried.

"How much of it do you think is propaganda?"

"What?"

"The papers. The books. How much is truth, how much window dressing?"

"Of course it's all truth! Red Cross reports back it up. What are you talking about, window dressing?"

"When you're wooing a girl, do you show her all your warts? Of course not. You hide your pimples under this." Dragan tugged Marko's beard. "In a couple of years, even you won't know what's really behind all that hair."

Marko slapped his hand away. "Ah, philosophize all you want,

53

but one of these days, my friend, you're going to have to climb down off that fence you're sitting on, before you're pushed off it — into the mud!"

He turned on his heel and walked off to join the crowd gathering around a speaker's podium decorated with posters encouraging Workers of the World to Unite. Half a dozen earnest young men and women wearing red armbands were handing out flyers to their fellow students. For a moment Dragan hesitated, tempted to join the group. He had attended the last rally held on the campus hoping to relieve his doubts about the practical applications of Party policy, but the speaker had ignored him, and his questions had been lost in the babble of chanted slogans. The strike the students' union had engineered had fizzled in less than a week. The romance of food baskets passed through windows and sleeping uncovered on hard benches hadn't really been worth the cost of the school closure or the beating Gligo had been pleased to inflict when his son came home.

Dragan turned and walked quickly away from the square toward home. Animated chatter faded to the clop of horses' hooves and the creak of wagon wheels. Dragan's thoughts moved from hazy political prospects to the more immediate issues of final exams and the search for a job. Much as he knew he would miss the farm, he felt a rising sense of excitement at the idea of a future in the city. Of course, he first had his military duty to perform. Although it was compulsory for all men over the age of eighteen, students, like only sons, were granted deferrals and shorter service periods. Dragan might be in for as little as nine months. And then, if he went to Zagreb, he could, perhaps, live with his older sister Dragica, at least until he found his feet and earned some money. If he decided on Belgrade ...

His reverie ended abruptly. He was home.

The day was unseasonably warm, and the bright sunshine had tempted Gligo to the restful shade of the plum grove. In one hand he held a cup; with the other, he twirled the ends of his ferocious moustache.

"Here comes the young Einstein!" he roared. "Join me, my learned friend. I am drinking a toast to our blessed King Peter." He raised the cup.

"Thank you, no. I don't care to drink," Dragan said. His chest felt tight.

Gligo's eyes narrowed. "What the hell do you mean, boy, refusing a toast to the king?"

Dragan gritted his teeth. A muscle bunched in his shoulder. "I'm not refusing the toast, I'm refusing the drink. I have work to do."

For all his bulk, Gligo could move quickly when he liked. He reached Dragan in two strides. He towered over the slight figure of his son. Dragan held his ground.

"Work?" Gligo sneered. "You and your *comrades* don't know the meaning of the word. Reading this trash is not work!"

He flung out his arm, knocking Dragan off balance and his books into the dust.

Gligo laughed as pages from *The Students' Voice* fluttered to the ground.

As he stooped to retrieve them, Dragan noticed the headline on the front page: "NEW HEAVEN ON EARTH IN SOVIET RUSSIA." His fingers tightened on the student card in his pocket.

ii

April 6, 1941 dawned sunny and warm in the capital. Thousands of people in pressed suits and pastel dresses thronged the marketplace, singing loud hosannahs in celebration of Palm Sunday. Outside the Church of the Ascension, a bride giggled with her bridesmaids, while her stern, proud papa tried to take their photo from the steps. On the other side of the square, a dozen Young

Communists staged a rally, their banners proclaiming support for the treaty Germany had signed with Russia just hours before.

Suddenly, the sound of engines filled the air and the sky grew dark with planes. To the people in the square, staring upward in shock, the black swastikas were clearly visible as the first wave of German fighters dove on the royal palace and heavy bombers began to unleash their deadly cargo on the priceless relics in the public library. Panic-stricken pedestrians scrambled for cover in crude bomb shelters, their shrieks of terror lost in the scream of the Stukas.

Invading armies had destroyed Belgrade thirty-seven times in the city's two-thousand-year history, but never with the shattering efficiency of the attack which Hitler had bluntly code-named Operation Punishment.

It was over in minutes. When the choking clouds of plaster dust cleared, a bomb crater marked the spot where the wedding party had stood. Around its rim, the torn, naked bodies of the bride and her attendants were strewn like the petals of a flower. A young woman suddenly old stumbled across the street carrying what remained of her infant son, crying and smothering his blood soaked little arm with kisses. The Young Communists were luckier. Their rush to help fight the fire blazing in a police warehouse was rewarded with boxes of the banned Soviet novel *How Steel was Tempered,* which they carried off to inspire fellow partisans in their fight against the Nazis. The flames from other fires raging out of control across the city were visible from the Romanian border, forty miles away.

Poverty and isolation had long ago doomed the southern Slavs to hatred and reduced their politics to near anarchy. So absorbed were the people in their own divisions—Croat versus Serb, Catholic versus Orthodox, Communist versus Royalist—that they filled their own powder keg. The Nazi occupation detonated it. When the Wehrmacht marched in, Yugoslavia fell apart. Italy,

Hungary, and Bulgaria all grabbed chunks of it but the largest piece of the carcass, a region openly sympathetic to the Nazis, became the Independent State of Croatia, with Ante Pavelich and his Ustashi army at its head.

The new bosses immediately outlawed the Cyrillic alphabet which distinguished Serb from Croat. They banned Orthodox Church rites. They began mass arrests of Serbs living in the new Croatian state. And by the end of May, the Glina massacres had begun.

iii

The first victim to fall in Petrinja was Dragan's cousin Simo. The two had eaten lunch together on the day Simo died.

"My treat," Simo said. He noted with approval the steaming bowls of goulash, the thick black bread, the brimming glasses of wine drawn from the spouted barrel in the corner of the tavern.

In the centre of the table lay a sales brochure featuring the latest model of the Singer Sewing machine. Dragan tapped it with a finger.

"How's business going?"

"Fantastic. Every woman in the district wants one of these babies for her dowry."

"Oh yes? How much do they cost?"

"Hang on to your shirt, cousin." Simo paused for effect. "Five thousand dinars."

"Each?"

"Each. And they're selling like hotcakes. Get one while they last and pay in instalments."

Dragan picked up the brochure and looked at it carefully. In the week before final exams at the teachers' college, the German army had invaded Yugoslavia and broken it into pieces. As the country erupted into a bloody civil war, Dragan's dreams for the future had collapsed. He needed a job.

"How big is your territory?" he asked.

Simo grinned. "The whole district. It's all mine. Between selling and collecting the instalments, I'm putting a few miles on the old bike tires, I can tell you."

"I'll say."

Simo winked. "Keeps me in shape for Milica."

Dragan laughed. Simo took the brochure from his hands and placed it in his pocket. He dropped a few coins on the table, then pushed back his chair. "I'm off."

Simo's bike was propped against a plane tree. Before retrieving it, he embraced Dragan.

"Thanks for lunch. My treat next time," Dragan said.

Simo laughed. "You'll never have the money. Teachers aren't appreciated the way salesmen are."

He was whistling as he pedalled away.

Three kilometres outside of town, the road curved sharply to the right around a knoll of parasol pines. The top of the knoll was a popular trysting spot for young lovers eager to escape the prying eyes of parents and neighbours. From the balding crown, one could watch, between kisses, as the sunset turned the clouds into a riot of pink and orange. Darkness descended in waves to the ground until, one by one, the stars appeared and the moon rose pale as an oyster shell above the trees. Simo grinned, remembering the last time he had brought Milica to the knoll. Neither of them had noticed the sunset at all.

A cloud of dust and the growl of an engine brought him back to the present. Someone was coming fast from the opposite direction.

"Probably a supply truck," Simo thought, pulling over as far to the side as he could to give it space to pass. What appeared a moment later was not a truck but an army jeep, driven by two men in the Croat Ustashi uniform. Each had one hand clamped around a bottle and the other on the steering wheel. As the jeep veered towards the left shoulder, the soldier in the passenger seat yanked the wheel hard to the right, sending the vehicle skidding to the opposite side of the road and provoking his companion to jerk it back to the left.

Alarmed, Simo pulled over onto the verge and stopped, straddling his bike, ready to leap off and dive for the ditch. The jeep swerved to a halt ten feet in front of him and the soldiers swaggered out of the jeep. Both were young, at most a year or two older than Simo. A few months ago they might have helped each other with the harvest, shared a bottle of *rakija,* played a game of soccer. Now there was hostility in their eyes. Confronted by their uniforms and guns, Simo knew before they spoke that he was not facing his neighbours, but an enemy.

"Let's see your papers."

Slowly, Simo got off his bike and drew his identity cards from his pocket. The smell of alcohol radiating from the soldiers made his nostrils twitch.

"What are you doing out here on your bicycle?" the driver asked.

"I work for the Singer Sewing Machine Company. I'm making my rounds." Simo was careful to keep his voice even.

"He's making his rounds," the driver repeated. His sidekick laughed as though he had been told a very funny joke.

The driver's eyes narrowed. "I've seen you before, salesman. Making your rounds. You travel all over the countryside, don't you? See a lot of different people."

His tone was accusatory. His companion registered the change and stopped laughing. He, too, regarded Simo with heightened suspicion. The driver unbuttoned his holster.

"You know what, salesman? I don't think you're 'making rounds' at all. I think you're making trouble. I think you're one of those Serb traitors going around stirring up revolt against the legitimate Croat government."

Simo shook his head. Fear had struck him dumb. Speech was the only weapon he had but his tongue was glued to the roof of his mouth. Desperately, he tried to loosen it. His words came out in a croak.

"No, I'm just a salesman. Look, I can prove it. I have all my receipts."

He reached for his pocket, then pulled his hand slowly back as the soldier drew his gun.

"Where are all your little Communist friends? Taken to the hills?"

Simo stared steadily back at him without replying, knowing there was no acceptable answer to the question.

The soldier smirked. "What do we do with Partisans, Janko?"

"We shoot them," his friend said.

Simo's lips moved in a silent prayer. He crossed himself as both soldiers pointed their revolvers at him and fired. Their aim was spoiled by the amount of liquor they had consumed and they needed several shots to bring their quarry down. They reholstered their guns and offered each other a congratulatory slap on the shoulder.

"Well done, Janko. It looks as though the Singer Sewing Machine Company will have to hire itself a new salesman. Let's see if he actually has any money on him."

They turned Simo's pockets inside out, collecting not only the dinars offered up as instalment payments but also the gold watch Simo had rewarded himself with on his first-year anniversary with the company.

"What do we do with him now? Leave him here?"

"No, no, Janko. What kind of message would that send? We'll see that he gets home safely."

They hauled Simo's body into the back of the jeep and threw his bicycle on top of him.

At the train station in Petrinja, a young boy dolefully kicked a soccer ball around the end of the deserted platform. He looked up as a jeep screeched to a halt beside the ticket office. Two soldiers got out. One of them yanked a bicycle out of the back of the jeep and heaved it onto the tracks, breaking the front wheel and several of the spokes. The bell on the handlebar trilled a single note that sounded oddly loud in the quiet of the railway station. The boy watched wide-eyed as the first soldier returned to the jeep to help his partner hoist a man's body out and dump it near the edge of the platform. He backed away, hoping to escape notice, but just as he turned to run, he heard a shout.

"You! Boy!"

The boy stopped and turned around.

"Come here!"

The boy took a few wary steps forward, his eyes on the soldier's face. He pretended not to notice the body lying on the platform.

"Closer!"

The boy moved closer, his eyes unblinking. The soldier pointed to Simo's body. "Do you know this man?"

The boy glanced down at his feet and nodded once without speaking.

"Do you know where he lives?"

The boy nodded again.

"Good. I want you to take a message to his family. Tell them their son is here at the station. Tell them they are to come and pick him up." He looked at his friend and grinned. "Tell them he missed his train."

iv

When the Ustashi began to round up the Petrinja Serbs, Dragan and his brother-in-law Ivo were harvesting hay. They had risen before dawn, when the moon still bathed the fields

61

with golden light and scythes effortlessly cut through the dew-moistened grass.

With the heat of the morning sun came a swarm of fat black flies. Their persistent buzzing made Dragan twitch.

"It's not the flies I hear, but your stomach," he said to Ivo.

At eight, they were hungry. By ten, the growling in their stomachs drowned out the meadowlarks, their shoulder muscles ached, and their backs gleamed with sweat. Dragan was about to curl up next to a haystack when he heard the wild jangle of a bell and looked up to see his sister Ankica bumping her way across the field on a bicycle, its front tire wobbling.

"Where have you been?" Ivo demanded. He gestured at Dragan. "The two of us are nearly starving to death."

"Ustashi," Ankica panted, "and Lyubica and Stevo have arrived."

Ivo dismissed his wife's cousins with a wave of his hand.

"Ustashi," he said. "What are those bastards up to now?" As a Croat himself, Ivo was under no threat from the Ustashi, nor was his wife. Her Serb family wouldn't enjoy the same immunity. "What's going on?"

"They've arrested all the Serbs."

Dragan's mouth went dry. "Mama? Papa?"

Ankica nodded. "Everyone. They gave them ten minutes to get ready — what can you get ready in ten minutes? — and then they loaded them up and herded them off to that abandoned factory at the edge of town. It's all right though, they'll be all right there."

Ivo said, quietly, "I've heard they're building a concentration camp near Zagreb."

"It's not a concentration camp," Ankica corrected him. "Internment only."

Wordlessly, the two men swung their scythes over their shoulders and started for home. Ankica pedalled unsteadily beside them.

"Dragan," she said, "the Ustashi know where you are. They say if you go to the collection centre and join Mama and Papa, nothing will happen to you. They say you will be quite safe."

Dragan said nothing.

Ankica continued, stubbornly, "All these stories about torture and killing, that's all they are, stories."

Ivo patted her arm.

When they reached their own well-tended yard, Ivo handed Dragan his scythe and motioned him go inside the house alone.

"I think I'll have a bit of a look around town. See what I can find out." He pulled Ankica's arm through his, like a fellow setting out for a Sunday stroll with his girl, and affected not to notice the soldiers who had taken up residence across the street.

Dragan found his cousins sitting at a dining table so well scrubbed the wood looked freshly cut.

He slapped Stevo on the shoulder and kissed Lyubica on both cheeks. "What in the name of heaven possessed you to come back here?"

When the civil war broke out Stevo's job with the local post office was terminated; Serbs couldn't work for the new Croatian state. He and Dragan had briefly discussed the possibility of getting jobs in Germany. Better to be employed there, they reasoned, than unemployed in occupied territory. But the Germans weren't yet desperate enough to hire Serb labour, so Stevo and Lyubica had headed for Belgrade. Stevo could work in the post office there; it was under German, not Croat, control. The occupying forces were in urgent need of local help, and they were happy to issue the legal passes that would make it safe for Stevo to return to Petrinja long enough to pick up his clothing, his furniture, and his brother Milan.

Stevo wagged a finger at Dragan. "Be thankful that they did. What we brought with us might just save your skin."

Lyubica pulled a sheaf of papers from the pocket of her skirt.

"Travel papers?" said Dragan.

Lyubica nodded. "Made out in the name of one Milan Kosovac. He was already gone by the time we got here so he won't need them."

The door slammed and Ivo entered the house looking grim. He put his hand on Dragan's shoulder.

"The neighbours are gone, Kostic and Karadjic both," he said. "Their families ... they've all been taken away. Their houses are empty but the Ustashi are watching them. The station, too. They're just itching for someone to make a wrong move. Don't let it be you." Ivo hesitated, then added, "They beat Karadjic to death."

He handed Dragan a train ticket. "It's Petrinja to Zemun, but obviously you can't get on the train here in Petrinja. All those guys know you, they'll pick you up in a second."

Dragan agreed. "I'll walk to Blinjski Kut and take the train from there, hopefully all the way to Belgrade. If I make it, I'll find you two there." Stevo saluted and Lyubica blew Dragan a kiss.

Dragan looked at his sister. "Ankica, you'll let Mama and Papa know I am safe?" She nodded, tight-lipped.

"We'll take a couple of hoes," Ivo said, "and head over to my vineyard. The Ustashi won't bother us if they think you're still helping me with the farm. It's far enough out of sight they won't notice you leave."

It was after one o'clock when Dragan slipped away from the vineyard and into the woods, climbing the overgrown, gently sloping carriage road long since abandoned by wagons but still favoured by lovers. He strained for the slightest sound but heard no ardent whispers, no trilling birdsong, not even the muted rustling of squirrels in the underbrush, only the distant tramp of booted feet and the grind of trucks changing gear along the road on the other side of the hill. His own feet trod noiselessly on needles fallen from the close growing pines that crowded overhead and darkened the woods even in daylight.

It was twelve kilometres from Petrinja to Blinjski Kut, through pine and aspen forest that dwindled now and then to clearings and open fields. Beyond the cool shelter of the trees the air was still. As Dragan hiked steadily north, the sun beat down on him. There was no track to follow as he crossed the meadow and timothy reached to his thighs while thistles caught at the hem of his trousers. He heard a faint, sweet call and, looking up, saw three birds circling slowly. A lifetime ago, on the track to the cemetery in Bijele Vode, he had watched another trio of birds perform the same aerial ballet. Then he had thought he might meet the ghosts of his brothers on the hill. Now he was about to become a ghost himself.

The sun was so bright it hurt to stare too long at the sky. Around him, the meadow grass shimmered. Sweat ran in a dark furrow down his back. Heat and thirst tugged at his memory until he was once again facing down a headstrong gander with a stone, while Ilija raced ahead to tell Mileva all about it. Dragan smiled grimly. He would have counted himself lucky if a willow switch was still the worst he had to fear.

At the far edge of the meadow, a pile of rock and rubble marked the remains of what might once have been a small farmhouse. Just beyond it, Dragan turned back up into the protection of the woods and stopped to rest. Pulling open his rucksack, he examined the food Ankica had insisted on packing for him. There was black bread, slightly dry after the trek through the open field, a few generous slices of *kielbossa*, and a handful of green onions. For dessert, a very solid, very sweet chunk of slightly tired-looking cake. Dragan ate a piece of bread and the onions, and carefully packed the rest back into his rucksack. Who knew when he would be able to find more food? Besides, if he ate it all now, he would only feel drowsy and he still had four kilometres to go.

Between bites of the sandwich, he took the identity papers from his pockets and sorted them. One was a student card— "DRAGUTIN METIKOS — GRADUATED JUNE 1941." Dragan frowned at it. All his dreams, all the years of hard work come to this. The diploma he was carrying with him into exile was not the one he had laboured to earn but a squib issued by the government to celebrate the founding of the Independent State of Croatia. All students in their final term were automatically graduated and the final exams Dragan had studied so hard to pass were never held. With a sigh Dragan removed his right shoe and tucked the student ID inside.

The second document read "MILAN KOSOVAC — AUTHORITY TO TRAVEL PETRINJA — BELGRADE ONLY." Dragan folded it carefully and placed it in his shirt pocket along with the train ticket.

His hand shook slightly as he tore into strips the final piece of paper, his call-up notice to the army. That part of his life was over before it had even begun. There was no Royal Yugoslav Army left to join. Holding the shreds of paper in his cupped hands, Dragan stood and flung his arms wide, scattering them like confetti.

As he bent to pick up his rucksack, he noticed that he had set it down on a patch of clover. On impulse he knelt and ran his fingers through the blossoms until he found what he was looking for: a single stalk with four rounded leaves. He plucked it, gently pressed it flat, and tucked into the pocket over his heart. Then, with a last look back across the field toward Petrinja, he turned and headed deeper into the woods.

γ

Dragan crouched behind a hedge of wild currant on the hillside above the train station at Blinjski Kut. It would be foolish to risk standing around in the open any longer than he needed to, but he didn't want to have to run for the train. Haste would only attract attention. He checked his watch for the third time in as many minutes. Six o'clock. In the distance, smoke from the approaching engine stained the evening sky. Dragan brushed off his pants and made his way down the hill at an oblique angle that would bring him out at the far end of the stationmaster's office.

Three men were waiting when he strolled unhurriedly onto the platform. They looked about the same age as he and were dressed alike in twill pants and open-necked shirts. All of them studiously avoided eye contact with each other or the two Ustashi who lounged against the doorway to the ticket booth. Dragan observed the soldiers while pretending to study his ticket, but the soldiers weren't paying any attention to the people waiting for the train. They were busy admiring the way the smoke from their cigarettes spiralled in the fading sunlight. The taller one kept reaching down to pat the pistol on his hip as though to reassure himself it hadn't disappeared from its holster while he inhaled.

A few minutes later a shrill whistle split the air and everyone shuffled into line at the edge of the platform. Dragan pulled his identity papers from his pocket, reminding himself that his name was now Milan Kosovac. A million men could have answered to the description of average height, average weight, and brown hair detailed on the papers. The conductor didn't give him a second glance as he mounted the steps of the train and took the first empty seat by a window. His heart stopped when a soldier in full combat uniform swung through the connecting door at the far end of the car. The man took a long hard look at the seated passengers and strode directly towards Dragan. He hesitated a moment, then, apparently deciding there was more leg room on the other side, settled himself opposite an elderly couple in rainbow-trimmed folk costume. Dragan exhaled slowly.

The soldier's seatmates had the look of a couple so long married they had grown to resemble each another. Their weather-beaten faces were lined and creased, and their faded eyes were set deep in a spray of wrinkles. Both had calloused hands gnarled and knotted by hard work and arthritis. The man was stocky, his neck bullish, and in his youth he would have been someone to reckon with. But now he was a tired old man. His wife was still handsome, as strong women often are in old age, and though her body looked as though it pained her, she held her back straight. There was an innocent pride in the way she smoothed the apron of her skirt and flicked imaginary dust from her husband's black trousers. The couple might have worn these same outfits to their own wedding. Their clothing had the carefully preserved air of garments seldom used but meticulously kept. The white shirts with their full sleeves had yellowed with time. They smelled faintly of goat.

The soldier spoke in a loud voice. "Where might you be off to in such fancy dress?"

"The festival at Zemun." She paused before asking, "And you?"

The unnecessary postscript earned a warning look from her husband.

"The front."

"Really. Which one? There seem to be so many now that we are fighting on the side of the Germans."

There was a collective indrawn breath throughout the car. The moment stretched. Dragan melted closer to the window. Why, he wondered, did fear always follow the same path through his body? Why didn't it make him go blind? Or deaf? Why did it always make a beeline for his bowels?

The Ustashi emitted an unexpected bark of laughter. "The Russian front, mother. I'm going to the Russian front. Ivan is about to discover the value of a German peace treaty."

Evening faded into night and outside the window the dying sun was replaced by a sheaf of stars. The train rattled and jerked along the track toward the Danube, that lifeline of central Europe, still winding its way peacefully across a crazy quilt of fields towards a yellow moon. Dragan dozed fitfully, sliding deeper into sleep only when the soldier disembarked at Zemun.

The festivalgoers followed and Dragan rubbed his thumb across the destination printed on his ticket, scoring his nail through the ink. There were only three other people still left in the car, two of them men he had seen on the platform at Petrinja. More refugees headed for the Serbian capital.

At dawn the train crossed the bridge over the Danube and came to a stop near the grotesque forest of debris that had been Belgrade's central station. The early morning sky was a turmoil of rose and saffron. Dragan thought of blood and sunlight on summer wheat. He stepped out onto what remained of the platform and nearly plunged headlong into a shell hole. When he recovered his balance, he was trembling. Sweat beaded his face. He felt encapsulated, the space in which he moved crystalline and empty, the ground under his feet undulant and insubstantial. A fine high keening sounded in his ears.

Though the details of Belgrade's disaster still lay in heavy shadow, its contours were clear. More than seven hundred buildings had been destroyed by the German aerial assault.

Dragan wandered through the ruins along Pariska Street, where cleanup had already begun. Rebuilding would happen slowly, men and materials being pressed into more urgent service. But the Byzantine ramparts that embraced the city, and the curving lines of Turkish influence in its architecture, endured. Shell-shocked peple picked their way through shifting dunes of rubble. The lilac bushes and flower gardens in Kalimegdan Park were shredded, the ground pocked with bomb craters, but the beautiful bronze by Mestrovic at the entrance still stood. By the time he reached it, Dragan's muscles were tired from the tension and hard walking. He felt the familiar tumult deep inside, emotional vertigo spiralling down through his gut.

He watched the sun roll up over the city.

NIGHTFALL

Leningrad, 1941

After a quick shuffling of seats and some nasty comments from the people behind them, Mama had blocked Galina's access to her cousin Lidya, effectively ending the tickling match that had provided the only entertainment in the theatre that drizzly May afternoon. Going to the movies was supposed to be exciting. Galina loved collecting the two-inches-by-two souvenir booklets sold in the lobby kiosk, a dozen pages of black and white stills. They were vivid reminders of the stirring scenes and romantic heroes portrayed on the screen. She stored them in the bottom of her mother's sewing basket, taking them out as mood dictated, to laugh at Walt Disney's penguins in their black and white tuxedos, or to fantasize over *The Great Waltz,* imagining herself in the arms of an aristocratic gentleman dancing under sparkling chandeliers in a ballroom.

Now Galina slumped in her seat, arms folded across her chest, and determinedly did not look at the movie screen in front of her. Today's feature was billed as a blockbuster but, in Galina's opinion, *If Tomorrow is War* offered little to lighten the atmosphere of the day. Outside, heavy grey clouds intermittently spit cold showers on pedestrians hurrying past the Aurora cinema. Inside, on the screen, massed tanks stirred up billows of dust and the drone of endless legions of silver aircraft made Galina's head ache. She shrugged off the *oohs* and *aahs* of appreciation from the audience at this reassuring spectacle of Soviet military might. For the past year and a half she had watched Uncle Nikolai pin little flags on the map of Europe he had tacked to his living room wall. With each visit to his apartment, Galina had noticed the circle of flags growing wider as the German army hacked its way across the continent, from the initial chop in Poland, to the gash across France and the Netherlands, to the most recent thrust into Greece and the Balkans. Germany and Russia had signed a non-aggression treaty, but the grumbles Galina had heard from Uncle Nikolai suggested not everyone put much faith in it. German troop movement to the Soviet frontier had been escalating all month; when, not if, seemed to be the question on everybody's lips. Many Leningraders, Mama included, might welcome the overthrow of the Bolsheviks and the end of executions and exiles, arrests, and the midnight knock on the door. But even she wasn't naïve enough to think that Hitler's Nazis were a better alternative. As rank upon rank of lean, hard-eyed Red soldiers marched across the screen, the audience cheered.

Nikolai muttered, "Don't they know it's just a movie?"

Galina stole a glance at him. Like all of her uncles, Nikolai had received his call-up papers. Even in street clothes, he had an air of distinction. Galina could only imagine how much more impressive he would look with medals on his chest. He was to leave for Azerbidjan in two days. Aunt Zina was already wringing her hands like a widow.

Galina sighed, wishing they could have seen the musical comedy *Tsirk* again. Now that was a movie! She kept its souvenir booklet by her bed and dreamed regularly of its glamorous star, Orlova, the big-eyed blonde with the dazzling smile. She liked Charlie Chaplin too, and the image of the Little Tramp cooking shoelaces into soup still made her chuckle. But even *The Gold Rush* keepsake had ended up with the others in the sewing basket. *Tsirk* had been special.

While artillery rolled by on the screen in front of her, Galina daydreamed. In *Tsirk*, Orlova had played a white American with a black child. She was banished from the United States and escaped to Russia to start a new life in the circus. Glittering musical numbers were rare in Soviet film; a black baby in the arms of a white woman was extraordinary. There weren't, Galina reflected, very many black people in Leningrad. In fact, they were quite a novelty. She had seen one last year. One day after school she and her friends had walked six blocks out of their way to investigate a ship docked in the harbour. The sentry was rumoured to be black. And what an awesome sight he had been, with his uniform so white against his dark skin. He wasn't nearly as cute as the baby in *Tsirk* of course, but still, a fine example of the people the great Paul Robeson had spoken of. Robeson's tour of the Soviet Union had certainly caused a stir. Galina and her friends had talked of nothing else for a week. What was it he'd said? Something about American blacks, as descendants of slaves, having so much in common with Russian workers, as descendants of serfs. It had certainly sounded impressive. Robeson had liked the Soviet Union. He said it was free of racial prejudice, and he had even talked of immigrating. Galina didn't think he had actually done that. The film director, Eisenstein, had arranged his tour and once it was finished, Robeson had returned to the United States.

Galina squirmed in her seat. While the couple behind her hummed the "Internationale," Galina hummed the theme from *Tsirk:* "I know of no other country, where a man so freely breathes." Maybe, she thought, if tomorrow there really is war, we won't have to watch this movie any more and we can see *Tsirk* again.

Guns weren't nearly as thrilling as the sight of Orlova leading a crowd through Red Square, a song of freedom on their lips.

ii

Galina loved the white nights of summer, when daylight dimmed in the midnight hours but never deepened beyond dusk. The white nights were when students from the university strolled arm in arm through leafy parks and their parents toasted the end of a long, dark winter with champagne parties on the Neva River bridges. She loved Sundays like this one. It was near the end of June, sunny and lazy, when she and Mama, Lidya and Ninulya packed a basket with sausage and black bread and took the train to Sestroretsk, where a sandy beach ran down to meet the Gulf of Finland. The girls chattered excitedly as they left the apartment. Soon there would be cool water on their bare skin and the warm softness of sand between their toes.

As they crossed the courtyard, Lidya bemoaned the worn condition of her sandals. She was describing the new white pair she had seen and coveted when she stopped in mid-sentence. The archway and the street beyond were clogged with people, the biggest crowd Galina had ever seen. Even as she wondered at the reason for it, a flat, unemotional voice sounded from the loudspeaker mounted on a telephone pole. In a few brief sentences, Foreign Commissar Molotov announced that German troops had attacked the Soviet Union. He mentioned Zhitomir, Kiev, and Sebastopol: "The government calls upon you to rally even more closely around the glorious Bolshevik Party, around the Soviet Government and our great leader, Comrade Stalin. Our cause is just. The enemy will be crushed. Victory will be ours."

Ignoring their protests, Nina quickly shooed the girls back upstairs. Then she joined the hordes of women who descended on the grocery stores like locusts, provisioning themselves against the approaching onslaught.

Twenty years of Soviet rule had taught them how to cope with

73

shortage and hardship. Cereals, canned goods, and matches flew off the shelves but, without refrigeration, perishables were out of the question. Besides, Nina thought ruefully, rationing made it difficult to stockpile. One hundred grams of butter didn't spread very far, especially on dry bread, and if the German army kept advancing, the rations would only get smaller. More than once, Nina mused, she had been forced to queue and re-queue before she had enough cold cuts for a party. How long would they be standing in line now for a cup of sugar or a slab of lard? She studied the orderly chaos on the street. Citizens whose monthly wage barely supported them in peacetime rushed to buy what-ever they could now that war had been declared. Outside the banks, lineups grew long. People took their rubles to the com-mission shops and turned them over for rings, watches, rugs, samovars, anything with hard value that they could later use as barter. Maybe those who believed the Red Army would stop the Germans were right, and all this panic was for nothing. But if the Soviet might failed ...

As August gave way to September, Peter's great city pre-pared to meet the enemy. His charger no longer reared on the banks of the Neva: the heroic statue had been shrouded with sandbags and cloaked in planking. The Klodt stallions had dis-appeared from the Anichkov Bridge, buried in the Summer Gardens under mounds of protective earth. Stone sphinxes still guarded the embankment, and bowed caryatids still shoul-dered their burdens on the threshold of the Hermitage, but rubbish was collecting in the gutters and the *prospekts* were grimy. Day after day, long columns of soldiers snaked through the city. Weary men who had survived one battle were on their way to another. A clear, blue sky curved like a saucer over park lawns and flowerbeds crisscrossed with trenches and packed with gun sites. The lindens that lined the wide avenues glowed purple and russet over spreading carpets of mushrooms. A bad omen, the babushkas said: Many mushrooms meant many deaths.

As the days passed and the German army marched steadily closer, Nina and thirty thousand civilians like her were drafted to dig trenches and tank traps. A small group of army sappers directed the work, but the brunt of it was borne by women who returned to their families at night exhausted, their clothes in rags, their bodies aching, and their hands raw.

Galina stood at the window and watched her mother climb down from the tram that had carried her from the front. Nina moved slowly, as though every step hurt. Even from a distance Galina could see that her clothes were black with dirt and sweat. As she turned to cross the room and unlock the door, Galina's eye fell on the framed photograph of her parents that stood on the desk. Though she had burned all his papers, Nina could not bring herself to destroy this picture of her husband. She and Sergei were smiling into the camera, he in the cap he always wore to hide his thinning hair, she young and eager, the smoothness of her skin and the darkness of her curls dramatized in a studio glow. Galina thought Mama looked like a movie star. When she stumbled into the apartment that afternoon, however, the film had spun along on fast forward so that the actor's hair now showed grey, not gracefully at the temples, but in all-over flecks. Her fine bone structure hadn't altered but there were lines around her mouth and eyes, and her skin had lost its lustre. Her expression was dazed.

"Mama!"

Galina supported her mother's stiff-legged progress to a chair. Fear coiled in her stomach and with the back of her hand she wiped the tears streaming from her eyes.

"Mama, what happened? Please, tell me what happened."

She had to strain to hear the monotone reply. "Their planes came flying very low. They were shooting at us. Someone yelled to get down, to put your shovel over your head to protect yourself from the bullets." Nina looked apologetic. "They were not very big shovels. And there were so many bullets."

The next day, she went back to her post.

iii

Galina and Lidya sat on the rooftop of the apartment building. They were surrounded by buckets of sand. Leningrad shimmered in the moonlight, each roof and spire clearly etched against the sky. Suspended in the air above were legions of antiaircraft blimps. From the ground, they looked like fat, grey sausages.

"They float like great white whales in the sea, don't they?" Galina said.

Lidya shook her head. "I think it's creepy sitting up here in the dark all by ourselves."

"No, it's not. It's exciting. And anyway, we're not exactly alone. Look, you can see the fire wardens on all the other rooftops. Just think, if one of the firebombs lands on ours, we can save the whole building. We'll be heroes."

"I don't want to be a hero."

"Well then, pretend you are a cat instead. Cats like to sit on the roof in the moonlight."

"I wouldn't want to be a cat these days, either. Anatoly Chulitsky's cat disappeared two days ago. The one he's had since it was a kitten? I think his mother served it to them for dinner."

Galina made a face. "Remember the day Uncle Alexei brought us a piece of dead horse from the front? That was nasty."

"Anatoly says you can practically spit to the front."

"He must have very strong spit. The front's at the end of the tram line. Mama goes there every day to dig trenches. You should see her hands!" Galina examined her own hands, noting with approval how soft and plump they were.

The shrill scream of a factory sent the girls scrambling to the edge of the parapet, where they watched open-mouthed as thousands of bombs dove like wingless hawks on the southwest quadrant of the city.

"The food warehouses," Lidya gasped.

The wooden buildings that held the city's food supply were set only thirty feet apart in a compound that covered several acres between the freight station and the locomotive depot. As the bombs exploded, dozens of fires, blindingly bright, ignited and spread. Galina could almost feel the panic of the workers as they raced for sand buckets amid the rattle of anti-aircraft guns and dodged swords of water from the fire hoses. In minutes, mountains of smoke crisscrossed by searchlights and floodlit by flame billowed into the sky. Inside the warehouses, tons of sugar melted and flowed into the cellars. Rivers of butter began to boil. Galina imagined the streets running with melted chocolate. Meat and flour to feed a city of three million souls were gone, leaving nothing behind but an acrid stench.

Galina and Lidya cowered on their rooftop. Showers of incendiaries slid down the thick walls of the ancient Peter and Paul Fortress before burning out on the sandy banks of the Neva. In the amusement park next to the fortress, there was a thunderous explosion and flames lashed the roller coaster. Beside it, the animals in the zoo began to shriek. The death screams of Betty the elephant echoed all the way to Vasilevsky Island. Fear-maddened sables escaped into the streets and in the Pavlov Institute the dogs howled like dirges.

Apart from her cousin's sobbing, Galina heard no human sound.

The First Long Range Artillery Fire on Leningrad

— Anna Akhmatova
(translated by Daniela Gioseffi)

A multicoloured crowd streaked about
And suddenly
all was totally changed.
It wasn't the usual city racket…
It came from a strange land.
True, it was akin to some
random claps of thunder,
but natural thunder
heralds the wetness of fresh water
high clouds
to quench the thirst of fields
gone dry and parched,
a messenger of blessed rain…
But this was as dry as hell must be.
My distraught perception refused
to believe it,
because of the insane
suddenness
with which it sounded, swelled
and hit,
and how casually it came
to murder my child.

From *On Prejudice: A Global Perspective.* Doubleday/AnchorBooks, NY (c 1993)

iv

At the outbreak of war, public broadcasts exhorted the city's residents to cover their windows with paper, to keep the glass from shattering under the shockwaves of bombs and mortar fire. In a matter of days, every window in Leningrad boasted some kind of artwork.

"Vera Michailovna has monkeys on hers, but I think elephants are better because they're stronger," Galina said.

A small oil lamp provided the only light in the room where she and Lidya sat cross-legged on the rug, combing each other's hair. Sitting together in the evenings saved fuel. They alternated apartments.

"I don't think monkeys would protect us nearly so well from bombs. *Ow*, be careful," Galina said, as Lidya jerked a brush through a stubborn knot.

Lidya started to braid her cousin's waist-length tresses. "I wish I had hair like yours, Galya. Mine goes all thin and straggly if it grows past my shoulders."

"They say if you cut it all off, it grows back thicker. Mama used to cut mine short every summer, remember?"

"So did my mother, but it doesn't seem to have made any difference. Maybe I should try shaving it all off and starting over. Though with my luck, it probably wouldn't grow back. Can you picture me at parties?" She laughed. "Ladies and gentlemen, may I introduce you to the beautiful, the talented and the very bald Mademoiselle Ustinovitch."

Aunt Zina said, "Lidya, I don't know how you can make jokes in times like these, with your Papa God knows where at the front and the Germans surrounding the city. What parties are you likely to be able to go to?"

Lidya bit her lip. Galina glanced toward the corner where her aunt sat mending socks. The fitful light made her expression

unreadable, but the whine in her voice suggested the lines of dis-
content and self-pity around her mouth would be etching themselves deeper. At her feet, her younger daughter lay curled like
a cat who had discovered that sleep was the only reliable escape
from the new realities of life.

In the curtained alcove that had once been Marusia's retreat,
Nina studiously ignored her sister-in-law as she picked through
their meagre store of food. It was a blessing, she thought, that
the army's call to duty had left one less mouth in the apartment
to feed, though Marusia had always been adept at stretching the
food budget. War-time rationing made it much more difficult
to be clever. Meat and vegetables had become luxuries enjoyed
by few. Now bread, in portions reduced to 250 grams a day, was
largely sawdust. What would happen once winter set in? Nina's
eyes flickered to the sturdy brown leather suitcase sitting in the
corner. The smudges and scratches spoke of a wedding trip, visits
to Luga, family vacations by the sea. Once it had held holiday
clothes and souvenirs. Now it was filled with emergency supplies, tinned fish, and dried fruit, enough to keep her and Galina
alive for a few days, at least, if the worst happened and their
apartment was destroyed. She patted the pocket she had sewn
inside her blouse to hold, and hide, their ration cards. If they lost
those, a bomb would bring a kinder death.

The door to the apartment swung open and a blast of cold
air heralded the arrival of Lily. She was carrying a few sticks
of wood, which she dumped on top of the small pile beside the
stove. Her once carefully sculptured pin curls were flattened
under a black felt beret. The days of cloché hats and fine leather
gloves were over.

Frowning, Lily picked a sliver out of her finger. "The trees on
the boulevard are disappearing fast. Everyone is stockpiling. If
we're lucky and the winter isn't too cold ..." The end of her sentence was drowned in the scream of an air raid siren.

Galina shouted above it, "I hate that sound! It's just like a dragon shrieking."

Lidya yelled back, "How do you know what a dragon sounds like?"

"Well, it's what I imagine a dragon sounds like."

"You and your imagination."

"Walt Disney made dancing penguins. Nobody insulted his imagination."

"I remember that movie. It was my favourite, next to the Charlie Chaplin one about the Goldrush. You know, the one where he cooks his shoelaces for dinner, like spaghetti!"

"He should see what we make supper out of now!"

Nina's voice cut across them sharply, "Will you girls stop nattering and get a move on? Galina, for goodness sakes, nobody cares what your hair looks like in an air raid shelter. Put on your boots!"

"Yes, Mama."

In a muttered aside to her cousin, Galina added, "Everybody knows it takes the bombers at least ten minutes to get here after the siren goes. The shelter's right next door."

"Galina!" Nina's tone was threatening.

Galina hastily shoved her feet into her boots and started lacing them.

Zina yanked Lidya up from the mattress by the elbow. "Don't just sit there, child, move!"

Lily, her arm around a yawning Ninulya, was opening the door into the hallway when the first bombs of the night jolted the city.

Galina still frowned over her boots. Rushing to the air raid shelter twice a night was becoming a bore. Initially it had been interesting to note, from one day to the next, who among their friends and acquaintances had been evacuated, or shipped to the front, or killed. But as time wore on, the pattern became repetitive. It was an entertainment dragged out in too many instalments.

Galina uttered a *"tchah"* of disgust. In her haste, she had missed several of the eyelets on her boots. She was just starting to take the laces back out to thread them again when her mother hauled her to her feet and hustled her out the door, not caring that Galina might break her neck over the untied strings before she reached safety.

Rough wooden benches lined the walls of the basement shelter and formed another square around its centre pillars. Galina squinted in the semi-dark. The benches looked full. Initially, all of the occupants had been friends and neighbours, but as the daily assaults continued, familiar faces gradually disappeared, sometimes whole families at a time, to be replaced by other faces and other families who had been forced from their homes and their neighbourhoods by bombs and shellfire.

Lily waved from a spot along the west wall. She shifted Ninulya onto her lap and scrunched closer to her neighbour on the left, leaving just enough space to let Nina and Galina squeeze onto the seat. Nina shook her head in exasperation.

"I don't understand this daughter of mine. She has absolutely no sense of reality."

She stopped short in her scold, throwing a protective arm around Galina as the building vibrated from the concussion of a bomb. Glancing up from her mother's shoulder, Galina noticed a girl on the middle bench opposite. Her pallid skin and the dark circles under her eyes made her age difficult to guess. Galina was shocked to recognize Tatiana, who had been two years ahead of her at school. Tatiana's mother had been one of the first victims of the siege, felled by artillery fire as she walked down the street. Now, of course, ubiquitous blue and white signs cautioned "CITIZENS: IN CASE OF SHELLING THIS SIDE OF THE STREET IS THE MOST DANGEROUS" and people simply moved to the other sidewalk.

Tatiana had taken over as the woman of the family, caring for her two younger brothers while her father continued to play the violin. The Leningrad orchestra continued to play Beethoven overtures at their concerts. The musicians were making a statement: even under siege they would play German music and draw strength from it. Meanwhile, the city's own musical genius, Shostakovich, was composing his brilliant Leningrad symphony and the whole city was waiting to hear it.

Tatiana's father was an accomplished musician. *Had been,* Galina corrected herself. Was it only a week ago that Galina had heard what had happened to Tatiana's family? The girl had balked at running once again to the bunker near her home. "It's too cold, Papa, and I'm too tired. Let me stay here," she pleaded. "I'll be all right, I promise. Take the boys, they feel safer in the basement." And her father had gone, leaving his precious violin in her care. Tatiana had fallen asleep, to be woken by an explosion and a chunk of plaster falling on her head. Through her window, she saw flames dancing through the clouds of dust and rubble where the air raid shelter had been.

Galina looked away from the huddled figure clutching the violin case and stared down at her boots. Her eyes widened in dismay. Not only were the boots not properly tied, they were on the wrong feet. She glanced furtively around to see if anyone else had noticed. She tucked her feet back under the bench. Beside her, Aunt Zina moaned softly, calling on her absent husband to save her and their girls.

Letter to the Front

To: Nicholas Ustinovitch (the father of Lidya and Ninulya)
Azerbidjan S.S.R. North Caucasus Military Region Kirovobad Post Office
(hold until called for)
Ustinovitch, Nikolay Petrovitch
Leningrad "2" Rubinshtine St. 15/17 apt. 607/7
Z.M. Ustinovitch

From: his wife Zina (Zinaida Mihailovna)

Leningrad, 11 October, 1941

Greetings dearest Kolen'ka!

How long you make us wait for your letters. The one promised in your telegram of 10/IX we received 9/X. The postcard for Ninulya (written 20/IX) came then also. Lidya was quite hurt that there was no word for her, you know how sensitive she is, and to make matters worse you did send a card to Ninulya. In your next letter to me, please enclose a special sentence or two for Lidya.

Life has changed completely since your departure.

We are all still in Leningrad, there is no way out—evacuation was stopped in August. So here we are. Lucky are those who got away, that includes you too. If only I could have foreseen what awaited us, I would have left everything and gone. But now, of course, there is no chance, it is much too late.

Since the end of August I have been assigned defence worker duties. I am frustrated and tired. I have no one to talk to and there is a constant struggle with the girls, as always. I am out all day, so they are on their own. If I try to say something, they argue, and you are so far away. The pantry is bare—we have to exist on ration cards, we have no other food. As yet, the girls are not in school, and we don't know when school might start. I do still have some money, since there is not much one can buy.

Recently, Lidya got paid for digging trenches (from 16th to 24/IX)— 33 roubles—and by chance, saw dress sandals that she fancied in the store. She begged permission to buy them, i.e. for me to add 71 rubles. Of course, I had to consent. She was delighted, her first earnings. I got a pair of white sandals for Ninulya too, and will shop for dress material on my day off.

Kolen'ka!, the money you sent on the 26th we got 29/IX and con-firmed by telegram 1/X, with second telegram 7/X. Considering the circumstances, I will send you telegrams at intervals, just in case, so you will know we are alive and well and you needn't worry.

Nina drops in from time to time, Niura is sewing her a dress. Serge was wounded and evacuated to Vologda. He recently sent a tele-gram that he recovered and got orders for Moscow, nothing more since.

Lesha is stationed near Leningrad, and has been to visit Nina (she told me) but didn't come to see us. Lily is working, I have not seen her since the end of August—no one has the time—we have to think how to get food and some rest. Vera Ivanovna Zaharenko (do you remem-ber her?)—she has been in jail since the 24th of August. She was told it would only be for a couple of days, but it looks like she lied again and now most likely will be sentenced for 2 years for sure. Niura was very upset at the start, but she has calmed down now. After all, it is all Vera's fault, the old fool, she should have known better. It's happened to her twice already—she has no one to blame but herself. Dubanev is in Leningrad and did call, so did Prokofii, and Melomedov visits from time to time. Fiodor does drop in now and then as well—I'm listing them off just so you know that all are near Leningrad except you, and we feel cheated. You are so far away, and there is no way to see you or talk to you—when we will meet again?

We get our ration cards at your office. Your co-workers always inquire about you and send their regards. Katerina Konstantinova received two of your cards and asked for your address—did she write or not, I don't know.

The weather is already cold, but dry. It does not rain too often—weatherwise, summer and fall were very nice. If only the radiators in the apartment would get warm!

Darling Kolen'ka!, please don't judge me too harshly if I sound negative, you know what I am trying to say. Write more often. The girls are writing to you—they have time—as for me, I go out daily to defence work, and no sooner do I get home than "the Germans start to bother us." For some reason, we were not disturbed tonight, so I can write a long letter. Don't blame me for my pessimism—I really have it hard—I do carry a heavy load.

Do write, awaiting your letters, greetings from the girls (they are already asleep).

Kissing you long and hard,
Zina

P.S. Ninulya is enclosing a card for you. Do write to Lidya—don't hurt her, she is working hard running the house and looking after Nina (I admit, sometimes she gets grumpy).

22hrs 40min 11/X–41

PARTISANS

Belgrade, 1941

❧

Dragan watched his cousin bolt the apartment door. Ear pressed to the wood, Stevo listened for a moment, then turned to face his three visitors: Dragan, his sister Dragica, and their friend Marko.

"It's all right. It was nothing."

His voice was even but Stevo's expression looked strained, the skin drawn tight around his eyes. He sat back down beside Marko, at a dining table covered with a dingy cloth and set with glasses and bread. No plates. Lyubica hovered with a bottle of *slivovica*, which she poured sparingly. Since the occupation had begun, supplies of everything were limited. Stevo and Lyubica were lucky they still had a roof over their heads. Refugees poured into the former capital, desperately seeking the protection of the Serb civilian authority, which was controlled by the Wehrmacht. To repay Pavelich's support, the Germans had recognized the Independent State of Croatia, but they were not quite as eager as the Croats to eliminate all the Serbs in the former Yugoslavia. The Reich was beginning to feel the pinch. It needed workers for its factories and fields. Regular sweeps of the markets and streets of Belgrade would help ensure a steady stream of cheap, disposable labour for the Fatherland. Resistance provoked reprisals at the rate of one hundred Serbs to every German killed.

Dragan pushed his glass away impatiently. "You want revenge."

Marko shook his head. "Justice. I want justice. I want to see those bastards cowering in the street. I want to smell their blood. You've heard what happened in Glina. You've heard about that death factory they've built at Jasenovac. Your own family's been sent there, for God's sake!

"Killing a few Germans won't bring them back."

Dragica put her hand on her brother's arm. "Dragan, don't you see? The only option we have is to fight. And the only place we can fight effectively is with the Partisans."

"What about the Chetniks?"

"*Pah!* Mihailovich is no leader. Even the British know it. They're throwing all their support behind Tito. He's the one with the guns and the guts to use them."

"Yes, I know," Dragan said. Now that Russia's sided with the Allies, all the world loves a *moujik*. But where were all these fighting Partisans when the Ustashi overran Petrinja? They took to the hills and saved their own skins." He glanced at Marko. His friend's nervous habit of playing with his beard had left small bald patches along his jawline.

"What else could they do, at the time?" Marko protested. "The fascists hate the communists as much as they hate the Slavs and the Jews. The Partisans had to fall back to gain strength and regroup. Speaking of which ..." he said, tapping his watch, "I have to go."

He made a small salute and let himself out. Lyubica relocked the door before sliding into the seat he had vacated. "Just remember, Dragi, it was the Croats who welcomed the Germans with open arms," she said.

Dragan shook his head. "We had Croat neighbours, classmates." He looked at Dragica. "Our sister is married to a Croat." He turned to Stevo, who was sipping *slivovica*. "What do you think?"

Stevo shrugged. "I've already thrown my lot in with Marko. We leave tomorrow."

Lyubica's eyes were bright with tears but there was a proud

smile on her lips. Her hand moved to her belly in a protective
gesture that was not lost on Dragan.

"Me too," said Dragica. "I'm going to fight."

"Even at the cost of reprisals?"

Dragica nodded slowly. "Even then."

Lyubica said almost rudely, "So what do you believe in,
Dragan? Not politics, apparently. Not revenge. What then?"

"I believe in staying alive. Look at you, the three of you are
so full of hate and self-righteous anger that you've blinded your-
selves to the truth."

"Which is what?" said Stevo. "What is the truth according
to Dragan?"

"The truth, cousin, is that in a fight we can't win. They're
stronger than we are. Whichever enemy you look at, they are all
stronger than we are."

"So you would do nothing?" Dragica's tone was scornful.

"What should I do? Say I see a man chasing a young girl down
the street. I know the man, I know his reputation is bad. I have
a gun in my hand so I kill him and save the girl. Is that the right
thing to do?"

"Of course it is!"

"How can you be so sure? All we really know is that the man
is dead. Or maybe only wounded since I'm not a very good shot.
A death has definitely happened. What would have happened if
I hadn't shot him, is something we'll never know."

"But the girl ..."

Dragan held up his hand. "Listen to what I'm trying to say.
I shot the man because of what I thought he *might* do. What if
I was wrong? What if the man was chasing the girl to return a
lost handkerchief?"

"That is such bullshit!" Dragica banged her fist on the table.
"This is war, Dragi, not a philosophy class. We all know damned
well that the man wants to hurt the girl. And in this case, Serbs

are the girl. We have to stop the man—Hitler, Pavelich, Mussolini—our goal is just and you know it."

Dragan stood up so suddenly his chair fell over. He leaned across the table toward Dragica. "Your goal may be unachievable and your means could create a future even worse than the one you envision now."

"Serbs don't want to live as slaves."

"No, but they do want to live. Your call to arms is inviting mass murder."

"And you think if you don't fight back they'll leave you alone?"

Dragan flinched at the contempt in his sister's voice. Stevo put his arm around Lyubica's shoulders and placed his hand over hers on her belly. He spoke slowly, "I believe there comes a time, Dragan, when fighting is the moral choice to make."

Dragan straightened, trying to ease the too familiar tension building in his neck and arms. He had carried the weight of an ill-defined anger all his life. He struggled to keep his voice even. "Killing leads to killing the way evil leads to evil. You want to do evil things today in the hope that something good will emerge from them. But between the present and the future, there's a long chain of cause and effect—and chance." He shook his head. "It's a wager that I'm not willing to make."

It was dusk when Dragan and Dragica left the apartment, rage still simmering between them. Down the block, a woman in a red kerchief disappeared into a doorway. The rest of the street was deserted. Dragan checked his watch.

"Damn! It's already six."

Dragica said, "Maybe we'd better go back upstairs. No point risking our necks by breaking the curfew."

"I have to get back to the barge."

"What, your sailors can't cook their own dinner for once?"

"Sure they can. But then they might decide they don't need me to cook for them and I'll be out of a job."

"So what? I can get you a job. A better job than working on a dredger in the middle of the Danube."

Dragan almost smiled. "You don't give up, do you?"

"Let me tell you something, little brother," Dragica said. "In war, many things are possible—valour, comradeship, heroism. But only for those who fight. For those who stand by, there is nothing."

A moment later, she had disappeared into the shadows.

Dragan's dark clothes blended with the scorched brick of the bombed buildings along the street. Over time, people had returned to the ones still standing. After clearing away the dust and the broken glass, they had hung their laundry out to dry and placed flowerpots on the windowsills.

Dragan spotted two civilian policemen a block away and ducked into a ruined storefront, waiting for them to disappear around the corner. He held his breath as a jeep full of German soldiers cruised past in the growing darkness. They waved their flashlights across doorways, more intent on getting to their supper than picking up curfew-breakers. Dragan sank deeper into shadow. Once the street was clear, he could continue to the Danube.

Traffic on the river had ceased for the night. Dinghies used to ferry workers from one shore to the other had been pulled onto the bank and turned upside down. They would make good cover for spies, Dragan thought. He gave them a wide berth as he made his way to the secluded jetty where, earlier in the afternoon, he had tied a battered rowboat.

A quarter of a mile downstream, the black bulk of a dredger loomed. Dragan glanced up, noting with satisfaction that a heavy cloud would soon obscure the rising moon. He waited for the right moment, then, crouching low, made a dash for the rowboat. He untied its painter and jumped in with the soft-footed grace of a cat. He pushed off from the edge of the jetty, letting the boat drift away from the shoreline before taking up the oars.

The screech of the metal oarlock echoed across the water like a clap of thunder.

There was a flurry of movement around the overturned dinghies on the bank and suddenly three German soldiers were running toward the river's edge. Dragan heard a shouted command to halt. He began to row faster, bending almost double as he tried to shield his body with the boat.

The order was barked out again, "Halt or we'll fire!"

On the edge of panic, Dragan reminded himself that in the dark, the soldiers could have no clear target. It would take time for them to set up a searchlight if, indeed, they had one. Once Yugoslavia had been crushed, Hitler had reassigned most of his troops to the Russian front, leaving only a token force, armed with poor equipment, to maintain order in the Balkans. The Germans banked heavily on the fact that the Serbs had nothing with which to fight back. Dragan took a final pull at the oars, struggling to put as much distance as he could between him and the soldiers.

The Germans' first shots were wide of the mark. Then a traitorous cloud shifted, allowing a shaft of moonlight to flicker through, and they readjusted their sights.

Dragan hastily shipped the oars and slipped over the side of the boat into the water. He kept one hand firmly on the gunwale and the boat itself between him and the bullets now spattering the water on the other side. He kicked his legs to stay afloat, remembering the lessons he had learned at Mrtvo More so long ago, and let the current take him beyond the of firing range to the safety of the dredger.

ii

Dragan's job as cook for the ten-man crew of the dredger included shopping for food as well as cooking it. He rose at four every day, when one of the men would ferry him to shore. With hundreds of others, he waited in line until the bakeries opened at six. There were days when the wait was in vain. By the time Dragan reached the doorway, the shelves were already empty. Meat was scarce, so were vegetables. Potatoes were the mainstay.

At the end of August, the teachers' college in Belgrade offered refugee students the chance to write legitimate final exams to qualify for teaching positions in the new Serbia. Dragan had abandoned his books along with his dreams when he fled Croatia, but now he saw a second chance at the future. He grabbed it.

The exams started on September first, a Monday so stormy that Dragan arrived at the college cold, drenched to the skin, and an hour late. He blessed the bad weather. Wind from the Carpathians always brought heavy rain at this time of year. It had slowed work on the Danube and the dredgers sat idle. Dragan wouldn't be missed for some time.

There were a dozen people engrossed in exam books when he arrived, dripping, at the door. He had no pen and no paper. The professor monitoring the exam stared at Dragan over the rims of his glasses.

"You look like a drowned rat, young man. Did you fall into the river?"

Dragan tried to smile but his teeth were chattering so hard he could only manage a grimace. The professor shook his head and rolled his eyes.

"Take that seat there, by the heater." He took a steel pen and an inkwell from his own desk and placed them in front of Dragan, along with an examination booklet.

"You have until noon." It was already eleven o'clock. Blowing on the fingers of his right hand to warm them, Dragan opened the booklet with his left and nearly shouted aloud. The first exam was an essay. Had it been a long list of questions, Dragan

93

doubted that he could even have read it through in the time allotted, let alone answered enough questions to pass. But an essay,
especially one about the literary giant Vuc Karadjic, was a gift.
The phrases "first Serbian dictionary," "collected folklore," and
"collaboration with brothers Grimm" sprang to mind even as he
fitted the pen into its wooden holder. He dipped it in the ink and
began to write.

Forty-five minutes later, he laid down the pen and stretched
out the kinks in his neck. The warmth from the heater, fitful
though it was, had dried his shirt and pants, but his socks still
clung damply to his ankles. Around him, papers rustled as the
other examinees signed their names to their work and closed
their booklets. Now that the first test was over, Dragan relaxed in
the knowledge that he had not disgraced himself with his writing. He looked around at the others, trying to gauge from their
expressions how they rated their chances of success. He grinned
broadly when he realized that he knew all of them; they were
former colleagues from Petrinja and Zagreb.

"It's practically a class reunion," he crowed, as one by one
they stood and slapped each other on the back, exchanging greetings and news from home.

"How is your family?" "They were arrested." "Safe, thank
God." "My father was shot." "My brother has disappeared, but my
sister is here in Belgrade with me." "In Jasenovac."

At the sight of one man in the group, Dragan put his hand to
heart before opening his arms wide for a hug. He and Lyuban
Polimac had shared the same school bench for nine years. From
youth to manhood, they had hunted tadpoles together, played
soccer, tested bottles of *rakija* and chatted-up girls.

"You can't go back and forth to the boat every night, Dragan,"
Lyuban said. "You'll get no rest, and if you're late next time the
professor might not be so forgiving. You'd better come home
with me."

Lyuban lived in a basement apartment, crowded with a narrow bed, a small table, two chairs, and a tiny sink that served as kitchen, bathroom, and laundry. The toilet was in the courtyard; he shared that with his landlord and three other tenants.

"It's not fancy, but it's home," he said. "I'm afraid you'll have to sleep on the floor, but I have an extra blanket and, even more important, I have these!" With a flourish, he pointed to a stack of books on the table. "Texts and course notes from our final year, how good is that?"

For the next four nights, the two of them slept very little, straining their eyes by candlelight to read aloud and quiz each other on the work. At dawn they left the apartment to queue for bread and walk to the college in time for each day's exam. By the end of the week they were exhausted, but happy. Both of them had passed; they were qualified teachers and now eligible for good jobs.

Their bubble burst when they were rejected from the teaching posts they applied for because they had not completed the mandatory military service. Dragan returned to the dredger.

By the beginning of December, ice was starting to form in the Danube and the dredger had to be moved to a side channel. By January 1942, the river was frozen solid.

Dragan moved into a one-room apartment, which he shared with four friends. By pooling their resources and frequenting the soup kitchens, they survived a bitter winter. The snowfall was so heavy that all public transportation was shut down for a month. Dragan and Lyuban went into business: they shovelled snow, chopped wood, sweated in a factory grinding soap into washing powder, and clerked for the Ministry of Refugees. The job market in Belgrade ebbed and flowed at the whim of the occupying army, and in the spring, Dragan went back to the dredger.

Food was still scarce in Belgrade, but Dragan had become so adept at scouring the markets that, even with his limited resources, he could sometimes purchase more than he needed for the crew. This he passed on to relatives who had drifted into the city with nothing but the clothes on their backs. Through them he learned the fate of aunts and uncles, cousins, and friends. His parents had survived arrest, the loss of their property, and shipment to the concentration camp at Jasenovac, where chance in the form of Uncle Dragutin had saved them. They were now living in a small village somewhere south of Belgrade. Dragan thought of them often. Although his happiest years had been the three years spent at Lokrum, apart from his father and mother, blood ties couldn't be denied. Dragan recognized in himself his parents' fatalism. Adapting to circumstance had been the pattern of their lives, and the model he now followed. Whatever the personal loss, whatever the political regime, Gligo and Mileva had long ago accepted that only change was constant. They followed the rules and hoped for the best. Their son would do the same.

Indifferent to men and their wars, the seasons unfolded as they always had. As fall touched the air with the first promise of frost, Dragan wondered how he would survive the coming winter. Much as he had the last one, he supposed. Meanwhile, his daily trips to the market continued.

The German occupation forces were sincere in their brutal promise of a hundredfold reprisal for every one of their soldiers killed. An officer had been gunned down as he supervised the loading of a truck with carpets, paintings, and icons looted from the remains of the National Art Gallery. He was berating the local workmen for mishandling the fragile goods when he was shot. He died with the words "clumsy Slav fools!" on his lips. The fool who shot him now faced the hangman.

There was no way for Dragan, on his way to buy potatoes, to avoid the scene. All foot traffic passed through the main square and the Germans corralled as many as they could into the space, forcing them to witness what they could not stop.

The ancient oak at the far end of the square had been converted to a gallows, with a rope thrown over one of its outstretched limbs. Beneath it, two soldiers held a man upright on a chair, a noose wound tightly around his neck. Against a brick wall, one hundred men, women, and children stared with terrified eyes at a phalanx of rifles and a truck-mounted machine gun.

A sergeant with a swagger stick and a gin-trap mouth stepped forward.

"This man," he said, aiming his stick at the tree, "has committed an act of terrorism against the German Reich, which lawfully occupies this city. He has murdered one of our brave young soldiers. He is not a soldier himself. He is a coward. Today all of you," he swung the stick toward the people trapped against the wall, "will pay for his cowardice."

He made a quick up and down movement, like a conductor waving a baton. The two soldiers holding the prisoner in place let him go and kicked the chair out from underneath him. In the same instant, the machine gun and the rifles opened fire.

Dragan felt his throat close. Beside him, a woman leaned over and vomited on the pavement, while her husband made the sign of the cross. Somewhere in the crowd a woman sobbed.

When the firing stopped, the German sergeant casually walked over to examine the bloody pile of corpses against the wall. Through a haze of cordite, Dragan saw him poke at one with his swagger stick. He watched the man unholster his pistol. Though the chatter of the machine gun still echoed in the square, the crack of the single shot made Dragan flinch.

The body of the hanged man swung slowly around to face the crowd, like an actor inviting applause from his audience. The man had been so badly beaten that his features were almost unrecognizable. His small beard, trimmed lke Lenin's, was crusted with blood. Around his neck hung a crude sign. It read "SPY SABOTER MURDERER."

SIEGE

Leningrad, 1941

The whine of incoming shells and the crash as they exploded no
longer had the power to terrify. Galina couldn't remember when
she had last enjoyed silence. The sound of destruction had become
the normal background to everyday life. Even inside the apartment, there was no avoiding it. Outside, one merely spoke louder.

"Lidya, stop dragging at my arm," Galina protested. "Mama
wants the water today, not next week."

"What's she going to do with it? And why is she scraping the
wallpaper off the walls?" Lidya was afraid she already knew
the answer.

"She's making soup."

"Out of wallpaper?"

"Out of wallpaper glue. It's made of flour, you know."

"Glue soup?"

"Pretend it's something else. Pretend it's borscht."

"Or chicken soup," Lidya said. "With carrots."

"And rice."

"And hot bread to go with it."

Galina walked quickly, Lidya clutching her elbow and hurrying to keep up as they threaded their way through the neighbourhood to the river.

Shell damage pocked the facades of many of the buildings
they passed and one had had its entire front wall blown off,

exposing its interior like the rooms of a dollhouse. The wallpaper and fixtures were still intact. Cobwebs of shattered electric wire hung from splintered poles and sagging cornices. To the west, the distorted fretwork of the rollercoaster was a hodgepodge of scorched and twisted girders.

The girls rounded the corner, then shrieked and flattened themselves against the wall as a bus veered toward them to avoid hitting a burning car in the middle of the road. A machine gun had been mounted on the front of the bus and soldiers were jammed into its carriage. It was only after it passed that Galina saw the charred animal carcass lying beside the car. From its size, she guessed it had been a horse. Scavengers were already busy with their knives.

The girls reached the river, filled their bucket and, carrying it carefully between them, started for home. The streets were crowded with locals seeking food or water or fuel, and refugees who had wandered in from other parts of the city. There were women in shawls with string bags over their shoulders, milk tins and buckets in their hands, children clutching cord-knotted bundles of bedding and clothes.

Overhead, a bomber with a swastika on its tail suddenly appeared, circled, and dipped low, weaving around the puffs of smoke from antiaircraft guns. People on the street stared as printed leaflets drifted down like feathers shaken from a giant pillow. Galina abandoned her side of the bucket handle and danced under the fluttering pages, trying to catch one. Lidya staggered under the full weight of the bucket and some of the precious water spilled onto the pavement.

"What does it say, Galya?"

Galina frowned. "It's a poem, Lidya." She read it out loud:

"Though it's getting cold / No need to grouse / What we send / Will warm your house."

She crumpled the leaflet in her fist and let it drop to the ground. "Let's go back through the park."

A few leaves still rustled on the trees, but most of the branches were bare. Underfoot, amber and amethyst had dulled and died and lay trampled in the mud. Frost had blighted the flowers no one had had time to cut. Their blackened stalks lined the gravel paths like tired sentries. Next to the empty fountain in the middle of the garden an enormous, unexploded bomb lay partially sunk in the earth. Sometimes people passing by touched it. Some spit on it. Someone had painted it with yellow speckles. It made Galina think of bonbons.

"People say it's filled with sugar."

A woman in a fur coat glanced at her sharply. "Flour would be more useful, daughter. Or meat." She turned to her companion and said, "They do say, though, that almost three-quarters of them never explode."

Lidya shivered. Galina ran her hand along the bomb casing, tracing a pattern in the speckles. Stamped into the metal were the letters e–y–c and the manufacturer's mark, "BUDERUS."

Letter to the Front

Leningrad, November 4, 1941

Dear Kolen'ka!

I received your telegram of 27/X on 30/X, but didn't reply right away. I meant to send my telegram as soon as I got the money, but it isn't here yet. Can't think why, will go to the post office today to make an enquiry.

Kolen'ka! I also got your letter of 28/IX on 27/X — you wrote that you would like to hear about our present life and how we are coping with day to day conditions. I did describe our life in my October 11th letter, you have most likely got it by now. I can only add that we are still alive and healthy. Every day we are exposed to danger, but as you see, so far no ill effect.

Recently, I started working in the factory at your company. There was no word from you for a long time, money was getting low, as were our general circumstances. I suppose you will send money, but we might not receive it (may get lost or some other reason), just as happened this time. Anyway, the work is not hard, I am getting used to it. The main thing is the food card — 1st category, labourer — this is most important nowadays (I could not have wished for more); the salary is 300 rubles. At first they offered me training, but later changed their minds, so I got a position as quality controller. The girl who was doing the job before me got a better paying position. As for me, 300 rubles is good enough. Besides, you are sending me some extra and there is nothing one could buy anyway but the daily ration. At the workplace I am being treated fairly, for now (how it will be in the future, I don't know).

I started working 28/X — 41 but didn't let you know because I wasn't sure how things would work out, but now it is all official. I was so tired of the constant work assignments from the housing authority — here I have my place, it is easier on my nerves. Plus, I do earn something in case you can't send us money on time.

*It was very hard to exist on two dependant ration cards until 1/XI.
Ninulya will hold a child's card til the end of the year, but a labourer's
card gives me 400 gr. of bread daily (twice as much as a dependant).
For the holiday, we got a chocolate bar each and nothing more, no
vegetables of any kind. Sometimes we do get some cabbage leaf soup
at the communal soup kitchen. One can get a second helping, but for
that you have to surrender your food card, leaving you nothing to have
at home.*

*6/XI—I continue. 4/XI part was written at work during my one hour
dinner break (to finish a plate of soup doesn't take that much time). On
the 5th I had no time to write, I got home after 5 (we work from 8 to 5).
The rumour is that soon we will be working an 11 hour shift—will have
to get used to that too, what more can I do.*

*Tonight, we didn't have time to finish supper—the alarm sounded
and during air raids we go downstairs to the bomb shelter under #11
house entrance. Andrei and Lena Fomishna don't go down—they are
very brave, they have no fear. I am afraid, not just for me, but for the
girls—if I don't go, they won't go. When I was doing defence work I saw
a lot—that is the main reason I do go down and the reason why I could
not finish the letter. This was a very active evening—we had to go to
the shelter several times. It must be because of the coming holiday,
they don't give us any rest.*

*23 hrs. 15 min. I am writing and listening for the next alarm.
Earlier tonight there was a meeting in the bomb shelter during one
of the raids—dedicated to the anniversary of the October revolution—
with every exploding bomb, the shelter shuddered and shook.*

*Lidya takes care of the house and shopping. She doesn't study. She
had headaches before, now they are getting worse, aggravated by mal-
nutrition and worry. All will be well—if we survive, there is hope.*

*These are very difficult times, there is no food, the market is bare.
There is some barter going on, mostly for bread. I had to borrow some
money from Lily (170 rubles) needed to pay for monthly ration and
the soup kitchen. Will repay when I get my wages.*

Dear Kolen'ka! Lucky are you and all the ones who got out of the city — we can only envy you. There is no way out for us. I have lost a lot of weight and am only half of what I was — I have had to tighten the belt quite a bit. To go through the same thing for the second time in my life — now the girls understand what you and I were talking about. They used to think it was funny. It is all very sad — it is beyond our power — maybe we will survive.

Nina is working for the time being. Lily has been to see us. Lidya stayed at her place overnight and had one extra meal out of it. I am grateful they don't forget me. Recently, Nina brought us some rice and cocoa butter, and Lily shared some cabbage and dry bread with me. I was not working at the time. I was very depressed and could not speak without tears. Now I am a little better.

The girls are writing to you on their own. Sorry that I can't write more often, on account of air raids. As I wrote earlier, Vera Ivanovna Zakharenko ended up in jail. Niura was visiting her from time to time. Not long ago, the end of October, she went to see her and was told she had been "discharged" on 8/X. Where to? No one knows. We think she must have died.

Ninulya started going to school in October, but not every day. It keeps her busy and distracted from grim reality.

So, til next time — forgive my clumsy letter, I was rushing to finish it before the raid alarm starts again.

Kisses, love you, will be waiting for your letters,

Zina

P.S. Greetings from all in the apartment. At work everybody asks about you and sends best wishes.

Lots of kisses, Zina

P.P.S. The money hasn't arrived. I have been to the post office and was told they will notify me when they receive it. It has been extremely long this time!!

iv

Winter arrived early and, briefly, Leningraders hoped that snow might defeat Hitler's army, as it had once defeated Napoleon's. Flurries blurred the scarred paint on the palaces lining the embankment, heavy coats were taken out of mothballs, and mothers cautiously anticipated reunions with their sons. Then the steel trap of German tanks and cannons surrounding the city snapped shut, severing the city's lifelines. Leningrad was cut off from the rest of the country.

A dream began to haunt Galina's sleep. In it, she floated out the window, past the marching paper elephants, toward a horizon the colour of red ochre.

An entire burning city was laid out before her, from the fortress island of Peter and Paul, to the dome of St. Isaac's Cathedral, and the gilded spire of the Admiralty. The pastel colours of what had once been private palaces were reflected in the ice on the river. Overhead floated silver barrage balloons and beyond them German planes circled the city like flocks of crows. The air smelled of snow and wet stone, burning paint, burning rubber, and something else. Galina wrinkled her nose as she strained to identify the sharp odour. Turpentine, that was it. Turpentine drenched the corpses that were carried past by the truckload. The harsh smell that lingered in the frosty air was the smell of death.

Galina stepped carefully around fallen rubble and shattered glass. The silence was so deep that each fall of her boots, each metallic squeak of leather on frozen snow, echoed in her ears. The wind stabbed her lungs as she drifted through the shadows of ruined buildings, past gaping windows and sagging roofs. Snow sifted down on her head and shoulders. With each step her feet felt heavier. On the *prospekt,* crippled streetcars and buses stood motionless in the snow like frozen dinosaurs. The city's procession of squares and boulevards had turned into a desert of ice.

She crossed the bridge to the Summer Gardens, where birch trees glittered, so laden with frost that they appeared to be in full leaf. On a bench, a man and a woman sat cuddled in frozen embrace, as though sleeping after a long walk. Galina wanted to sleep too, but some restless impulse kept her walking through the shadowy world of cold and snow and wind.

Down the parade she glimpsed a man carrying something heavy in his arms. He walked a few paces, rested, walked, and rested again. His burden sparkled in the shifting light. As Galina drew closer, she recognized the body of a girl. The man's daughter? A sudden eddy of whirling snowflakes blinded her, and when they settled, the man had vanished and Galina woke to find her pillow wet with tears.

In those days Galina woke reluctantly, never knowing where dream ended and reality began, certain only of the deadening fatigue that dragged at her mind, and the baggy eyes and growing pallor of illness that stared at her from the mirror. But each morning, her mother dragged her out of bed to stand in a long queue of frozen ghosts waiting for a slice of bread or a handful of millet. Nina was still on defence duty; she trusted their ration cards to her daughter, knowing that the soup kitchens would be empty long before she finished work for the day.

In the winter of 1941, Leningrad was a grey, granite city ruled by wind. Wind whistled in and out of drainpipes. It whirled snow up in clouds around doorways. It hurried people along the Nevsky *prospekt*.

When Galina stepped into the local soup kitchen, a woman was swearing loudly at a thin little boy who sat on the floor, ravenously chewing the hunk of bread he had snatched from the counter. "My ration!" the woman screamed. "He stole my ration!" The boy continued to stuff bread into his mouth, heedless of her shouts or the blows she rained on his head. Galina quickly thrust her own ration deeper into her pockets.

Out on the street again, she wound her scarf even more tightly around her head and neck. She remembered how she used to love to turn her face up to the winter sky and catch fresh snowflakes on her tongue. But now a pall of smoke wrapped the city in a dingy, unforgiving blanket and the falling snow was grimy with it.

Muffled in their winter clothes, people grew blind to the growing number of corpses in the street. There was no wood for coffins; they needed it for heat. The dead were wrapped in swaddling cloths like the mummies of ancient Egypt and left frozen in alleyways and parks, outside the cemetery gates, and along the banks of the Neva.

City water had long since stopped running, the mains burst under the impact of German mortars. Galina struggled through wastes of drifted snow to fill her bucket at an ice hole, ignoring the abandoned shrouds waiting for the river to thaw and carry them away. Even filtered through gauze, the water tasted terrible.

It was easy to die that winter. Half a million citizens the bullets had missed starved to death. Or froze. Some simply lost the will, lay down on their beds and didn't get up again. In December, Vera Michailovna joined them. Her neighbours came to touch her waxen cheek in farewell and to scavenge whatever useful bits of food or clothing they could find in her apartment. Paper monkeys still swung arm in arm across her bedroom window. On the bed beneath them, the dead woman lay dressed in her best dress, washed and carefully combed, her face empty of expression. Galina had seen that blank look before, at the funerals of her grandmothers. She wondered where the personality that had once animated Vera Michailovna's body had fled.

A small white terrier, Wolchek, whimpered in the corner, bewildered by the loss of his mistress. Yuri Andreyevich said loudly, "Let me have the dog. I will take care of it." No one believed him. The old man had a lean, hungry look and there had been no meat to be had for weeks. All of the dogs and cats had disappeared from the streets; even the crows had vanished. Yuri Andreyevich backed quickly from the room before anyone could snatch the dog from his hands.

Letter to the Front

Leningrad, 14th of January 1942

Greetings, my dearly loved Kolen'ka!

At present we are alive and well and waiting for letters from you. Life here is very difficult but we keep hoping for improvement — maybe it will come in time.

As of 23/XII – 41 I am no longer employed. In all, I worked for 2 months, but now there is no electricity and besides, the entire factory has been shut down. At home there is no light, no heat, no water — one can't get kerosene — and most of all, there is a terrible lack of food. This is the most unbearable part — many have died from starvation and just as many have frozen to death.

I didn't write on the 15th — it was very cold in the room and I didn't feel too well.

16/I Our daily routine: we get up at 10 – 10:30 and boil water for tea. At 4:00 – 5:30, again tea or some sloppy substance called "soup" (if we are lucky to get it) — that and 200 gr. of bread per person a day. It is better now; we used to get only 125 gr. We toast our bread, spread some mustard on it and have our tea. No sugar or sweets. Our only wish is for bread and thick hot porridge, something to alleviate the hunger pangs. Rumours are that the supply of provisions will improve soon. It is easy to speculate, but how it will be in reality?

So to say, we are still alive, but growing weak (skin and bones). I think we will make it, the most difficult times are over. In the shop where I worked, they are now making small ovens — burzhuikas — got one for us, very handy, works like a samovar. As a matter of fact, I use the samovar pipe, light it in the kitchen and then take it into the room to get a little warmth. We have pulled two beds together and sleep all three in a row, it is warmer this way. The weather is very cold — there is severe frost — we are all weak. We go to bed early — the room is cold and dark — we have no petroleum or candles. Besides, there is nothing to do

*and in sleep one does not think about food. We haven't undressed since
September the 8th, at first because of air raids and now because of the
frigid cold. We are surrounded by filth and dirt—it is disgusting
—when will be the end to it all?—I am exhausted.*

*December 8th I went to military headquarters and signed up for
evacuation as family of an enlisted man. They promised to help—I
chose Tashkent. Have had no word to date—was told that we will be
notified three days before departure. I did write to you about evacuation
in the telegram.*

*Elithaveta Aleksandrovna is inviting us to join her for a respite
in the village (Katya is also there with Shurik). Will write to her, to
enquire about food availability etc. Maybe we will go—we live and
dream. Who knows when the railroad will start running? I have no
idea what to do—the girls want to get out of the city. So do I. Just to go
someplace where we will have something to eat! If only we can stay alive
'til the railroad starts running—*

*Dear Kolen'ka! Write and tell me what you do and how you live.
It is hard for me to write, my hands are frozen—I hope you can read
my writing.*

*Marfa Fomishna died of starvation 22/XII–41—she was swollen.
(Some have swollen bodies, but we don't show signs of swelling as yet.
We eat a morsel twice a day and drink just a little). Others are alive
for now. Nina is working in the accounts department. Galya keeps the
house. Lily is also working at times, as always. We have heard nothing heard from Serge. Lesha is near Leningrad. Lily sends him parcels
and he sends her bread and canned food sometimes—once a month they
share with us what they get. If you could have been here, we would have
had it easier. Oh well, maybe we will be together again one day and will
live as before.*

*Kolen'ka! write to us, we only got your postcard of 16/X on 1/XII and
nothing more but a telegram once a month. We did send you a telegram
on 27/XII, and again 7/I, did you get them?*

The girls send their greetings—they miss you. As of 1/I Ninulya is

no longer in school, it is too cold, the classes are not heated — so much
for study. Lidya is in charge in our household. Every day she goes to the
communal kitchen to stand in the queue for bread and soup. I am stay-
ing home — my heart is too weak, I try not to exert myself too much —
I do tire very easily.

   Have to stop writing, my hands are numb from cold.
   Do write, we kiss you many times,
   Ninulya, Lidya, Zina

γ

Thick frost covered the apartment windows. Only the sound of
artillery fire still proved the existence of a world outside. Block
by block, Leningrad was disintegrating and hundreds of thousands of its citizens were homeless. Galina's home was still in one
piece, but the hot water heater installed by its Soviet builders
no longer functioned. Galina, Nina, and Lily packed what they
could carry and crowded into the apartment with Zina and her
girls. Zina's lips thinned to a martyred line when they arrived; a
husband serving at the front ought to guarantee her living space.
Galina pressed her back against the tiled wall of the fireplace,
willing warmth into her bones.

   Most of the furniture had already been split for firewood.
There were no curtains on the windows; they were needed for
bedding. Nina and Lily struggled with the weight of an empty
bookcase, angling it across the doorway to the small dining
alcove to lend the illusion of privacy to what now served as the
toilet. Tin cans served the purpose for urine; solid excrement
froze so quickly it could be thrown outside into the street, where
growing heaps stained the snow like dried blood on a handkerchief. The stench would be unbearable come spring.

   Hunger gnawed at Galina. Her mother had plundered their
emergency supplies so often the old suitcase was now empty.

They were fighting for survival on the official daily ration: a single piece of bread. Galina counted minutes obsessively, angry that her mother insisted on dividing the meagre allotment into tiny portions throughout the day. She longed to forget the pain of her empty stomach, to feel deliciously full even for an hour. Aunt Zina allowed Ninulya to gobble her entire ration at one time. But 200 grams of bread can't satisfy a growing child for long and the little girl was soon crying again. Hunger drained the energy from them all. Nina's hands trembled with effort as she cut the last of the antler buttons from her coat to boil them for the marrow. She consoled herself that her daughter was still healthy enough to stand in the soup lines, though there wasn't much soup to be had.

"We need water, Galya," she said.

Galina didn't mind going, there was no joy in the apartment. Uncle Nikolai had come back from the front with an arm missing and no medal to show for it. Lily had cut the empty sleeve from his coat and sewn the hole over. Nikolai wore the sleeve as a hat. Their faces pinched and blue, Lidya and Ninulya lay curled together like puppies, shivering uncontrollably. Zina lay beside them, staring vacantly into space. She hadn't spoken for two days.

"I'll be back soon, Mama," Galina said, pulling on an extra pair of mitts, though on a windless day it was not much colder outside than in.

Anonymous bundles of clothing moved along the boulevards on unsteady legs. Some of them struggled to pull sleds behind them, splashes of yellow and red paint bright against the dreary landscape. No laughing children rode the sleds, only shrouds, or those soon to need them. Metal runners squeaked in protest on the snow.

It was no longer necessary to go all the way to the river for water. A burst water main had created an enormous, half-frozen lake in the street a few blocks from the apartment. Galina joined half a dozen others who were chopping holes in the ice with small picks. Their movements were laboured. Nobody spoke.

Galina filled her bucket only half full and staggered as she lifted it. She tucked the pick back into the belt of her coat so she could grab the bucket with both hands. As she bent to take a better grip on the handle, a sparrow dropped like a stone beside her, frozen to death in mid-flight. For a moment, Galina was stunned. She glanced around to make sure no one else had noticed the bird, then stooped to stuff it into her pocket. She licked her lips in anticipation.

Shelling had started again and Galina stumbled toward the other side of the street. According to the posted signs, it was safer, but everywhere there were shattered walls and gaping windows. Piles of corpses lay in the street, some wrapped in rugs, others in curtains. Here and there, an arm or leg had escaped its shroud and jutted out stiffly from under the snow. Galina stared at the body of a small child tied in wrapping paper and bound with string like a Christmas present. A few steps later, she tripped over a pair of feet protruding from a blown-out doorway.

Peering into the gloom, she saw two men crouched over the body, and with a flash of understanding she knew they were cannibals. Officially, such people did not exist, but everyone knew Leningraders who had grown desperate, and young children were seldom seen alone on the street.

Galina grabbed the pick from her belt and brandished it as she backed away from the door. She was sobbing by the time she got home. She leaned against the building to regain her breath, and took grim comfort from the familiar smoke-blackened bricks. It was several minutes before she found the strength to climb the stairs.

vi

Uncle Nikolai slept upright in the only remaining chair in the apartment. Nina and Lily shared the bed, while Galina, Lidya, and Ninulya lay crowded together on the mattress in the corner. Their faces were scarcely visible under a mismatched jumble of coats, hats, scarves, boots, and mittens. Their shallow exhalations hung in the air like a mystic aura. One could imagine that the icy clouds were spirits from the other side.

Galina wondered drowsily if it might be Aunt Zina, come to watch over her children. A week ago, Lidya had snuggled close to her mother, seeking warmth and comfort. Instead, she found a body grown stiff and cold while they slept. Lidya had shaken her by the arm. "Mama! Wake up Mama! Mama, wake up!"

Her howls had roused Nikolai from his stupor. He had risen stiffly from his chair to kneel beside his wife's body. Awkwardly, he touched a cold hand to her icy cheek. Then, with a sigh, he gathered his daughters to him and held them while they cried.

In silence, Nina pulled the cloth from the table and with Lily's help, wrapped Zina's body in a makeshift shroud. Nikolai took the belt from his coat to tie it. Galina watched in silence while the three of them wrestled their burden out of the apartment and down the stairs to become part of the growing mound on the street.

The idea of Aunt Zina returning from the dead shrouded in a supernatural fog seemed no more fantastic than any of the bizarre realities of life under siege. Galina wondered if Lidya or Ninulya would find any comfort in the thought, but they were fast asleep, so she couldn't ask them.

She didn't know whether it was hours or only minutes later when the air raid sirens began to blare again. Time had very little meaning any more and the sirens had long since ceased to impress her. What was the point of dragging oneself out of bed? It was the only place there was any hope of being warm. It was the only place one could at least pretend not to be hungry, or frightened.

Across the room, Nina prodded Lily out of bed and tapped Nikolai on the shoulder before turning to Galina. Vaguely, the girl was aware of her uncle and aunt pulling her cousins, both practically weightless, from the mattress, and of her mother shaking her by the shoulder to wake her, but she was deliberately lost in a dream. Her family was together again. They were floating down the river, she and Mama in white summer dresses and Papa laughing as he guided their little boat under the arch of a bridge and through to the sunlight on the other side. Dimly, she heard her mother's voice pleading with her, cajoling her to get up. Galina coiled herself into a ball and did not respond.

She felt the weight of her mother's body beside her, the reassurance of her arms and the whispered breath on her cheek.

"What difference ... Everything is gone ... We can at least die together."

The bomb blasts moved inexorably nearer. Galina's eyes opened. Through the paper-covered window, she could see the flickering light of new fires. She curled her body more tightly into her mother's and waited.

vii

A confused mass of men, women, and children gathered at the Finlanski station under a watery April sun. They waited patiently to board the convoy of trucks would take them from their besieged city, and their patience was enforced by the line of armed soldiers who prodded them into a semblance of order. Everyone looked tired, gaunt, and weak. Some were so close to death they could barely stand. Each guarded a tied bundle or shabby suitcase, all of the past that the authorities would allow them to carry into the future.

In the middle of the crowd, Nina, Galina, and Lily clutched their luggage and each other. That they had survived so long and were still together was a miracle in itself. What had happened to Nikolai and the girls, they did not know. In the chaos of the bombing run that had devastated their neighbourhood the three had simply vanished. Lily had stumbled back to the apartment dazed and incoherent.

"We were together. Then a blast threw me against the wall and I lost hold of Ninulya. Everyone was screaming and crying and trying to get out of the basement. People were throwing bricks aside to make an opening. I saw them, I know I did. The girls were clinging to Nikolai."

Nina bathed her sister's cuts and ignored the wild look in her eyes.

"We must hope for the best," she said. "Nikolai is a good soldier."

They didn't speak of it again. Every ounce of energy they had was spent on survival. But by the end of March, Nina was slipping away. Her body began to swell; her skin took on a yellow hue, and the bones of her face stood out in sharp relief around her thin, bloodless lips. To add to her misery, she had diarrhea.

"Galuchka," she whispered. "Go to the cupboard. There should be a bottle of castor oil still on the shelf."

Galina stumbled through the gloom in the apartment; there was no oil left for light. Hands outstretched as though she were blind, she felt her way to the cupboard and ran her fingers along the shelf until she found a bottle. She squinted at the label, but couldn't make it out. Well, it must be the castor oil; there was nothing else left. Clutching the bottle tightly in her right hand, she used her left to guide her back to where her mother lay propped against some pillows. Galina undid the cap and handed over the precious liquid. Nina took a breath, screwed up her face in anticipation of the taste, and swallowed. Even in the gloom, Galina could see the surprise on her mother's face.

"What is this you've given me?"

"Castor oil, Mama. You asked for castor oil."

"This isn't oil, Galuchka. It's ... it has to be glycerine. I'd forgotten it was there." Nina laughed weakly.

Galina stared, uncomprehending.

Nina said, "Drink some, Galya. We may survive after all."

Rumour eddied through the city. The ice road across Lake Ladoga would soon begin to soften and the authorities were extending the evacuation lists, trying to move as many people as possible out of Leningrad. They were especially eager to be rid of citizens who might be tempted to join the enemy. If the Germans succeeded in taking the city, they would find no sympathizers. Those slated for evacuation were given no choice, their ration cards simply revoked. They left or they starved. For the first time since Sergei's arrest, his family thought that being on The List might be a good thing.

Ration cards were distributed in ten-day increments. Decades, people called them. When Nina tried to collect their cards for the third decade of April, she was told they were no longer eligible for rationing.

Lily quietly started gathering their things.

"What do you want with all that?" Nina said. "Let's just go. What good are photographs and jewellery? And just when do you plan to serve dinner with that silver?"

Doggedly Lily kept packing. "You'll be glad of these things one day, Nina. See if you're not. Meanwhile, here, put these on." She indicated a small pile of skirts and dresses.

By the time they left the apartment, they each looked as though they had gained two sizes.

Galina adjusted herself for the umpteenth time. "I have so many layers on, how am I ever going to go to the bathroom?"

She stepped over an unwrapped body on the stairs. The strength of the living had long since ceased to meet the needs of the dead. In any case, what might serve as a shroud could better serve as clothing.

In the foyer, two corpses propped against the wall watched sightlessly as the three women passed. Galina danced a small pirouette around the last one and, as she went out the door, she was humming the waltz from *The Snow Maiden*.

The decrepit passenger train ran slowly along the track from Finland station to the shores of Lake Ladoga some fifty kilometres to the east. The evacuees were abandoned on a siding where they awaited the next stage in their journey.

Galina stood quietly in line, listening to the snatches of conversation that eddied around her. Nina and Lily watched anxiously for their signal to board one of the open trucks.

A woman's high-pitched voice said, "Do you think it's safe, the ice road?"

"Would they be calling it the road of life if it weren't?"

"It has to be safer than the city."

"What else can we do? We have to take the chance."

A whistle blew. The line moved forward. Evacuees crowded into the trucks, climbing awkwardly over tailgates and settling themselves on their own boxes and bags. The soldiers prodded them to move faster. Galina clambered aboard, then reached down to Tante Lily for the suitcase. Lily handed it up and scrambled in after it. Behind her, Nina slipped and fell to her knees, knocking her head sharply on the edge of the tailgate. The line kept moving forward, threatening to crush her.

"Mama!"

A soldier hauled Nina unceremoniously to her feet and lifted her into the truck. Another slammed the tailgate shut. "On!" someone shouted and the vehicle began to move.

Galina and Lily anxiously inspected Nina's forehead, but the cold was so intense that the blood marking the cut over her right eye had already congealed.

The ice road across Lake Ladoga stretched past the horizon between high white walls thrown up on either side by snow scrapers. An endless column of trucks moved along its length in both directions. At each kilometre mark, an officer in a white cape stood ready with white and red traffic flags. Half-shelters made of ice blocks offered rough protection from the wind and, in some, the comforting glow of a fire was visible. At longer intervals, the ice-block construction extended to repair shops and camouflaged antiaircraft posts. Here and there lay the carcasses of broken vehicles, some still burning, some half obscured by ice and snow. Oncoming trucks simply detoured around them. No one stopped.

As the afternoon wore on and darkness fell, the traffic officers abandoned their flags. Guided now by the signallers' tiny green and white lights and the glimmer of their own flickering headlamps, the trucks moved steadily through a surreal landscape toward the far shore.

Galina's teeth chattered. Even crowded together as they were, three dozen bodies did not generate enough body heat to counteract the bitter cold. This year, it seemed, there would be no end to winter. Galina noticed one old man in the middle of the group, wrapped as tightly as a mummy. His wife tried her best to rub life back into his face, but the telltale red and white frost marks on his cheeks were a clear sign he wouldn't live through the night.

Someone said, "They say there is food on the other side."

"And a warm room?"

"Oh, of course. And what are you willing to trade for that, sister?"

The woman's reply was drowned in the drone of an airplane engine and the answering chatter of antiaircraft fire. Huddled behind the tailgate of the truck, Galina watched as one of the trucks down the line behind them exploded.

It took ten hours to travel the fifty kilometres from one side of the lake to the other. Twice they stopped to shovel the drifting snow from their path.

On the eastern shore, they joined thousands of others wandering the icy, rutted streets of a tiny, war-beaten village while they waited for the next stage of their journey to begin.

A simple wooden platform served as the train station. Next to it, Nina, Lily, and Galina shivered in yet another lineup, this time outside a cluster of rudely constructed sheds that housed the local evacuation authority.

"Mama, I'm tired. Can't we lie down and sleep somewhere?"

"We need food first, Galuchka. We can sleep later."

A small scuffle broke out. A woman ahead of them in the line keeled over, dead before she hit the ground. The same cold, hunger, and exhaustion that had killed her marked the faces of all the evacuees, leaving no room for pity. Two women tussled briefly over the dead one's coat and scarf, then they rolled her body into a snowdrift and reclaimed their places in line.

Family by family, the column shuffled into the first shed. Armed soldiers directed them toward one of two desks. Seated behind the desks, officials from the Department of Security, wearing padded jackets, felt boots, and fur hats with earflaps, warmed their hands on steaming glasses of tea. Galina's stomach clenched at the sweet aroma. She noticed that regular soldiers drank from tin mugs.

Nina fumbled through layers of clothes to produce her passport and order for departure, and laid them on the desk beside a heavily stamped list of names. Grudgingly, the man behind the desk put down his glass. His eyes reminded Galina of black currants set in unbaked dough. He pursed his lips as he matched Nina's documents to the information on his list. As far as Galina could see, there were no details written next to the names on the list, but there must have been code numbers to indicate each evacuee's status. She imagined theirs designated them as enemies of the state.

The official sighed and looked up with his little currant eyes. "Leningrad must be overrun with potential collaborators these days. We have been shipping you east for weeks. I think even Siberia will soon be overcrowded." His gaze sharpened on Galina.

"Siberia's not a very hospitable place for a young lady like you. Perhaps we could think of something else to do with you."

He leered, revealing a mouthful of silver teeth. Galina shrank against her mother. Nina put an arm around her and glanced at one of the soldiers. The official shrugged and held out a small sheaf of food coupons. Nina stared at them in shock.

"Citizen! So few? But —"

The official narrowed his eyes. Nina grabbed the coupons and hurried Galina out the door, Lily close behind.

A nearly full moon bathed the street in a pale yellow light. The thermometer outside the soup kitchen still registered below zero; inside, workers ladled hot kasha into bowls and the evacuees eagerly clutching them nearly swooned from the steamy fragrance of the room.

Galina started spooning kasha as fast as she could swallow.

"Galya!" Nina grabbed her bowl. "Not so fast. It'll make you sick."

"But I'm so hungry!"

"I know. We all are. But it's been too long since you had proper food. Your stomach can't take it. Go slowly. Don't eat too much at one time."

The room was crowded with people sitting on suitcases and crouching on the floor. There were no beds, no matresses. Beside Galina, a woman doubled over with stomach cramps. Nearby a man began to retch. Galina slowed her eating even more.

The wail of an animal in pain echoed across the room as a young mother rocked her two-year-old in her arms. She clutched him fiercely to her, as though hugs and keening could restore life to the small dead body. Families on either side huddled closer to each other and pretended not to hear.

Galina's fitful slumber was broken by the rumble of a train. The room was instantly abuzz as people checked their belongings and counted their children. Had any died during the night? The mad scramble inside the barracks was checked at the door by unsmiling guards, who once again directed people into orderly lines. Outside, a black steam engine dragged ten cattle cars to a wheezing halt. Long sliding doors stood open to receive their load and the evacuees struggled to climb aboard. One old man, too weak for further effort, sank to the ground. Those next in line stepped around him. The young woman who had lost her child in the night still clung to his body as she stumbled to her spot on the train. Galina linked arms with her mother and her aunt and they held their luggage close as they clambered into one of the cars.

Running wall to wall on each side of the doorway, plank shelves served as beds, tables, and seats for fifty people. In the centre of the car, a tiny tin stove offered feeble comfort. Its chimney sleeve snaked overhead to run out one of the two small high windows on the side.

A young couple with three frail, sickly children claimed the empty spot on the bench beside Galina. The father walked with a heavy limp and sagging arm that Galina guessed had sent him home from the front. His wife was white with exhaustion. She struggled to settle her two older children while soothing the baby in her lap. Galina screwed up her face at the fidgeting three-year-old, making him laugh. His sister, perhaps two years older, simply stared. The mother smiled shyly and leaned closer to Galina, as though to pass on an exciting bit of gossip.

"I heard that the rail lines to the north have been bombed."

"Where will they send us then, if not to Siberia?"

"South."

Galina turned eagerly to her mother. "Did you hear that, Mama? South! We might be going south!"

The guards slammed the doors of the cattle cars and bolted them into place from the outside. The light in the car dwindled to grey.

CAMELS SPIT

The Caucasus, 1942

Though the car door remained partly open while the train was in motion, there wasn't enough air to freshen a space where thirty-five people still slept, ate, and relieved themselves. Two more shrouded bodies lay next to the opening, waiting for the next stop.

There was room to stretch out now, a luxury, Galina thought, to be able to lie down to sleep. She glanced at the mute figure beside her, Tanya Fedorovna, who in the three weeks since they had boarded the train, had lost a father, a brother, and a baby sister and had yet to speak a word or shed a tear. Her mother, Svetlana Andreyvna, chattered almost incessantly in an effort to break her daughter's silence.

Lily dozed in an untidy heap of clothes, her legs resting on her suitcase. Nina tried to heat a pot of water on the tin stove that worked only sporadically.

The train stopped. Someone hammered on the door and slid it partially open.

"Any dead? Throw them out now!"

Galina blinked in the sudden glare. The snow was nearly gone. Tiny bluebells waved among shoots of grass along the verge. In the woods beyond, the trees shimmered with the green-gold of spring. Four men too weak to pick up the bodies by the door simply rolled them out before the train moved on.

Nina poured tepid water into a cup. "Drink, Galya."

Galina took a sip and offered the cup to Tanya, who did not respond.

Svetlana said, "I can't get used to it. No matter how often — just throwing them out beside the track like that — "

"You know it's only sense," Nina said. "Not disrespect."

"I dream about it sometimes, what happens to them after. I wonder if there are wolves, or cannibals."

The train stopped again and the door slid fully closed, cutting off the narrow shaft of light. Galina heard the bolt slide into place. They moved on slowly.

"We must be coming to a town," Galina said.

"They won't want us — dead or alive," Svetlana said. "We're invisible, so they can pretend we don't exist." She examined the two small chunks of bread in her hands. "And soon, we won't."

She ripped one piece of bread in half and forced it into Tanya's hand. She looked at the other half.

"Supper," she said.

Half an hour later the train stopped yet again and the door was unbolted from the outside; it slid all the way open.

"Mama, I have to go."

"Be quick then, Galya. And stay close to the train."

Galina nodded impatiently. She and eight others jumped to the ground. Along the length of the train, evacuees squatted beside the rails, unconcerned with privacy. Their guards watched them impassively.

Galina took a deep lungful of air. The fields and forests on either side of the track had a fresh, clean look that made her itch for a bath. She longed to take her hair out of its lank braids and scrub it until her scalp tingled. As for her dress, it would never be blue again. Luckily, it still fit. She fingered the dingy collar, wondering how long it would be before she might have something new to wear.

They had pulled onto a spur line, which meant they had been shunted aside to let more important traffic pass. It happened all the time. Galina had no idea how far south from Leningrad they had travelled; she only knew that wherever they were going, they were getting there very slowly.

A whistle shrilled in the distance. Galina shaded her eyes with her hand and stared down the track toward the oncoming train. There was an excited shout behind her and she turned to see half a dozen peasants materialize from the woods laden with baskets.

"Mama! Food!"

Nina climbed stiffly from the train carrying an armful of dresses. Svetlana jumped out behind her. Lily stayed behind to guard their remaining store of barter goods.

The oncoming train thundered past. All of its cars were bolted shut and armed guards stood on the rear platform.

"More soldiers for the front," Svetlana said.

"More fodder for German cannon," Nina said.

A peasant woman with strong hands and a hard face stepped closer, displaying her wares. "Meat! Real meat!"

Galina began to salivate. Their meagre ration of bread and soup had been easier to supplement by barter with the locals the farther they travelled from the front, but nothing ever seemed to satisfy the longing for a full stomach. The dresses her mother carried might pay for some carrots, a few potatoes, and a loaf of bread. Meat would cost more. Those with jewellery and silver did all right, but the lucky ones who still possessed the eternal hard currency of vodka always fared best.

Nina looked at her daughter. How long had it been since she had had a proper meal? She was fifteen years old and still had the body of a child. She was still dressed as a child, too. Nina insisted on the wide collars and pigtails; people were kinder to children than adults. But the girl needed strength to survive and who knew how long it would be before they saw meat again. Nina twisted the gold ring from her finger.

"Oh, Mama, not your wedding ring."

"What use is a ring if I am not alive to wear it?"

The engine let out a groan and a puff of steam. Evacuees and the free hurriedly concluded their exchange of treasures while the guards shouted and gestured with their rifles. The train began to roll slowly backward off the spur.

They had been travelling for more than a month when they reached Stalingrad. In all that time, the train had never reached full speed. There was always another delay to wait through, another detour to slow them. Time hung suspended, the days endless and empty. The guards grew indifferent. Why, Galina didn't know. Perhaps they felt that watching over passengers too weak to care no longer mattered. What did matter was that the door finally stood open. Warm May sunshine flooded the car and Galina stared open-mouthed at the shining white city of Stalingrad. It glistened on the banks of the Volga like snow in the clear, bright light of winter, burning the eyes.

The train came to a final stop at Armavir, on the edge of a vast collective farm bordered by a riot of red and yellow poppies.

ii

Galina's stomach fluttered. To calm it, she lifted her face to the sun and imagined she was a little girl again. She was at Businka's dacha in Luga, where the warm earth had felt so soft under bare feet and the white bark of birch trees gleamed against the sky. If she tried, Galina could hear the voices of the village children calling her out to play. She started when her mother pinched her cheek.

"Pay attention."

It took all day to sort out the two hundred and fifty people who had survived the trip from Leningrad. While soldiers matched papers to records and records to lists, a group of Cossacks waited impassively beside a motley collection of wagons, ready to transport the refugees to their new quarters.

Harnessed to each wagon was a horse, an ox, or a camel. Galina could hardly believe it. She had seen camels in the Leningrad zoo, but she had never imagined one of the odd, ungainly creatures could be used to pull a wagon. She shuffled closer to one. The camel fixed her with an arrogant eye, but did not stop its rhythmic chewing.

"Don't they look like hairy sphinxes when they're kneeling?" Galina said, stumbling a little over the unfamiliar word but proud that she remembered it. She had read about pyramids and pharaohs in one of her grandfather's books. "I hope we get to ride behind one of them."

"It looks like you'll get your wish," Lily said.

The driver tapped the camel with a long stick and yanked on its headrope. The creature emitted a groan that sent Galina into fits of laughter. Nina quelled her with a look. As they passed beside it on the way to the wagon, the camel spit.

It was dusk when they set out from the Alexandrovka station and fully dark by the time they had gone two kilometres. Night reached out and swallowed the little caravan. Galina felt like a blind girl stepping into an unfamiliar room. She held a hand in front of her face and wiggled her fingers, sensing their movement but not seeing it. Disembodied sounds eddied across the vast, flat landscape that surrounded her: the low murmur of voices, the squeak of a wheel, the groan of a camel. Invisible blossoms filled the air with a rich, sweet scent, heavy with mystery. Then the clouds shifted, transforming night into a thing of forms and shadows. From the black dome overhead, stars fell like rain. A pale moon lit up the cart track and glimmered on whitewashed walls in the settlement of Razshivatka. A dim pool of light in the window of a small house beckoned the newcomers. Galina stumbled out of the cart and followed Nina and Lily inside.

They were led into a small parlour furnished with two narrow beds and a table. Their landlady, a mother of two widowed by war, held a candle aloft long enough for Nina to wrap sheets around straw-filled mattresses. Galina fell into sleep revelling, for the first time since leaving home, in the luxury of a bed.

She woke to the raucous squabble of sparrows in the yard. For a moment she lay still, waiting for this dream to end and the air to fill again with the rattle and screech of the train. She turned her head to look cautiously around the room. Mama and Tante Lily were quietly rearranging their few belongings, making their suitcases into dressers. Lily was bemoaning the threadbare state of her clothes.

"This dress can't take much more wear," she said, shaking her head over a frayed hem. "And this tea, by the way, is undrinkable. Where did you get the water? I've never tasted anything so bitter."

Nina sighed. "There's a well just outside there. But I guess they must only use it for animals and washing. It's certainly not fit for humans."

They discovered that only one well in Razhivatka offered drinkable water. It became Galina's daily task to make the two-kilometre round trip to fetch it.

Venturing outside for the first time, Galina discovered the source of the perfume that had beguiled her the night before. In Leningrad, acacia bushes bearing clusters of yellow flowers abounded on the boulevards. Here the streets were lined with full-size trees laden with similar blooms, only larger and creamy white. Every tin-roofed house and thatched-roof hut seemed to have its own quota of acacias in front of it. Each also had its own large barrel beside it, but the arid climate of the region could hardly fill any of them with rainwater. Down the road, a cluster of bare-footed children eyed the stranger on the doorstep with suspicion. But curiosity soon overcame shyness and it wasn't long before her new friends were happily instructing Galina in the local do's, don'ts, and where is whats.

iii

Razshivatka was a *stanitsa,* a Kuban Cossack settlement. Its one hundred homes, its store, its school, its pharmacy were all replicated in the other *stanitsas* that bordered this collective farm and others scattered across the countryside. It was fitting that the refugees from Leningrad had come to roost there. The Cossacks themselves were a dispossessed people, descended from the legions of warrior-peasants whose cavalries had long defended the tsars. Originally bands of runaway serfs and adventurers, they elected their own leaders and built strongholds on river islands in the "wild country," a no-man's land beyond the control of any government. They protected the southern borders of expanding Poland and Muscovy, later called Russia, in exchange for freedoms and privileges that distinguished them from the enserfed peasantry. Napoleon said he could have conquered the entire world with Cossacks in his ranks. Fanatically devoted to the tsar and the Orthodox Church, renowned as fierce soldiers with unparalleled skill on horseback, they had rebelled against the Bolsheviks in 1917 and proclaimed an independent republic. But when the civil war was over the Soviet regime had abolished the Kuban government and revoked the Cossacks' traditional privileges. Resentment still burned hot.

The broad plain of their home in the northern Caucasus was bounded by water and stone. To the northeast, the Volga flowed into the Caspian Sea and, its mirror image to the west, the Don made its way to the Sea of Azov. Beyond the huge collective, prairie rolled briefly into foothills before the southern mountains thrust their craggy peaks skyward. In Razhivatka, seeded fields stretched endlessly to the horizon, and at night the only sound was the moan of the wind. The wind filled Galina with a nameless dread. It sent clouds scudding across the moon like black furies, and bowed the branches of the trees until they groaned and curtseyed like a chorus of demented witches.

Nourishing food and a quiet atmosphere soon restored the refugees to health. Three weeks after they arrived, Nina, Galina, and Lily were deemed fit enough to work. They were assigned to a brigade of weeders, all fellow Leningraders. Dawn barely stained the horizon when the ox-cart first stopped in front of the house to pick them up. Settled behind the driver were four local women wearing kerchiefs tied low over their foreheads. Their aprons bulged with roasted sunflower seeds and popcorn. The women nodded good morning. With no check in the flow of their chatter, they popped handfuls of seeds in their mouths, manipulating them with their tongues and cracking them with their front teeth like parrots, before spitting the shells onto the floor of the cart. Galina was fascinated. Eagerly, she accepted an offer to try the snacks and found that cracking seeds successfully was more awkward than it looked. But the popcorn was an instant hit.

The ride across open prairie was long and made slower by the crossing of several streams. The oxen had minds of their own. If they felt like wading through the shallows cart and all rather than crossing by the bridge, they waded. If the cool water felt soothing to their cloven hooves, they stood bathing in it for uncounted minutes while the locals continued to gossip and chew. Eventually, though, they delivered their cargo to the brigade leader, an elderly Cossack who was a man of few words. He simply handed out hoes and pointed to the fields that needed weeding.

Anxious to prove themselves, the three new hands diligently hacked at every green shoot that dared show its head above ground. The sun grew hot and the unaccustomed exercise made the women sweat. They took off their dresses, folded them into a neat pile, and continued their labours dressed only in panties and bras, pleased to be reducing both laundry and body temperature.

They were startled by the sudden appearance of a woman running across the field waving her arms at them and shouting: "Stop! Stop what you're doing! You're ruining the carrots!" Breathless, she explained. The Cossack was embarrassed by the ladies' undress. He wouldn't speak to them himself. But they had to be told: not everything that is green is a weed. It was the city dwellers' first lesson in farming and by the time they had learned it, it was noon. With an old piece of rail for a gong, the field cook hammered out the message that dinner was ready. Chunky soup and crusty bread were followed by a two-hour siesta, during which the locals slept in the shade of the cook shack, while the northerners lay out in the sun tanning themselves to painful shades of lobster.

All the able-bodied men in the *stanitsa* had long since been shipped to the front. They left behind illiterate women, old men, and young teens. Knowing their education set them apart, Nina and Lily were eager to earn their keep in other ways after their poor showing in the carrot patch. Nina became the brigade statistician, riding the fields in a two-wheeled cart to measure and calculate the earnings of the workers. Lily became the dairy bookkeeper, which meant she brought home milk and cheese home at the end of the day. Galina tried her hand at being a nanny. Other girls might not mind handling the infants' pacifiers: slimy gruel tied into knots of cloth, or washing and changing endless dirty diapers. For Galina, it was torture. Besides, she could barely lift the chubby darlings. It was back to the fields for her.

Workers on the collective were paid in kind, according to productivity, at the end of the harvest. But they still had to buy their daily bread and other necessities. What little money Nina had was gone, Lily's too. Yet luck smiled in the shape of their brother Alexei. Just as he had sent them horsemeat from the Leningrad front, now he sent army wages. Initially, his salary had gone to his wife and daughter. But the town they lived in had fallen into German hands and Alexei's pay was transferred by proxy to Lily.

To Nina's chagrin, there were no cigarettes for sale in Razhivatka. There was, however, some rough, homegrown tobacco available through barter with the Cossacks. They were delighted to teach this pampered northerner how to roll her own in a piece of old newspaper. The resulting "goat's legs" looked nothing like the cigarettes Nina was used to and their foul stench made Galina's eyes water, but Nina and Lily became regulars in the smoking corner.

Bathing was a problem, too, until Nina managed to barter an old wooden trough to use as a tub. Thereafter, baths and laundry were timed according to the landlady's baking schedule. When she heated her oven for bread, Nina filled the tub and Galina and Lily grabbed every utensil they could find, warmed them all on the hot bricks and threw them into the water. Tepid was the best they could hope for, but it was better than icy. They shared a toilet with the landlady and her children: a hole in the ground dug some distance from the house and enclosed by a fence of sunflower stalks. Meals were simple and they cooked them in the yard, where they balanced a pot on an iron tripod over a fire. Wherever they went, each of them carried a cloth bag to be filled with twigs and wood chips for the fire. Once in a while, a neighbour might offer space on her outdoor oven and in turn, Nina or Lily would help her write a letter or unravel red tape. By the end of summer, Galina was running barefoot with the other teenagers, riding horses bareback to the river, and raiding the watermelon fields for the ripest, sweetest fruit. She had been accepted as one of their own, and, like them, ever fell prey to scabies which had to be healed with a salve made of lard.

Most days, the war seemed very far away, the illusion of peace shattered only intermittently by the wails of mourners when someone learned of a fallen husband or son. People in Razhivatka knew little of what was happening on the front. The local paper painted a rosy picture that no one believed; its pages were used to roll smokes. Galina was getting ready for school when the war caught up with them once more.

iv

The German summer offensive began at the end of June 1942. A week later, Army Group A crossed the Donets River. On July 25, Rostov-on-Don, the gateway to the Caucasus, fell. By the end of the month the Germans were only a few days' march from the Caspian Sea. The speed of their advance during the early days of Operation Blue was a grim reminder of their success in the early months of Operation Barbarossa. The feeling grew that if the Germans were not stopped now, they would never be stopped at all.

Panicked, Stalin issued his infamous Order No. 227: any soldier who retreated or left his position without orders to do so would be shot. "Cowards" were assigned to *shtrafbaty*, special penal battalions which were used as human minesweepers: the entire unit was deployed across a suspected minefield.

"He can scream 'not one step back!' until a crayfish whistles," Lily said, "but how many soldiers is he willing to sacrifice?"

Nina shrugged. "How many citizens in Russia?"

It was late August when a German plane fell out of the sky over Razhivatka. Galina's eyes burned at the sight of the crippled silver bird trailing white plumes of smoke as it plummeted earthward. Behind it drifted a single silken parachute. Galina thought, "How lucky he escaped." Then she saw the dangling body twitch.

An instant later she heard a gunshot and her heart contracted as she watched the stricken flier crumple to the ground in her neighbour's yard. She ran to look.

Though his face was pinched with pain and fear, the boy reminded Galina of a fairy-tale Raslan. Villagers gathered to stare as though he were an exhibit at the zoo. Someone said, "He's asking for a drink." Galina thought, "He's asking for water." An image rose in her mind of a cool, clear stream rushing down a mountainside and a laughing boy running beside it. Her neighbour scurried into the house and brought back a cup of milk. Again Galina thought, "He wants water," but she said nothing. She wondered if the boy's mother would ever learn what had happened to her son or know that his dying wish had gone unanswered.

Rumours began to swirl. Propaganda posters arrived in advance of the army. The face on them was unfamiliar to the locals, its small moustache insignificant compared to that of Comrade Stalin.

"Who's that?" an elderly woman demanded of Lily, stabbing at the picture with an arthritic finger.

"Adolf Hitler," Lily said. "He's sending his army to free us of the Communists."

The old lady nodded in satisfaction. "Then he is a good man," she said and tacked his picture to her wall.

The rumble of guns drew closer and the night sky was full of flame. Razhivatka woke to the roar and dust billows of tanks on both sides of the creek: the Russian army was withdrawing from the front. Its commanders were garrisoned in houses, its soldiers in a tent camp nearby. The major lodged next door was frank: if they didn't get the order to retreat, the army would be surrounded. The local administration had already been told to evacuate the collective farm.

"What are your chances?" Nina said.

He shrugged. "I've got a suitcase ready with civilian clothes in it and the appropriate papers."

"What should we do?"

"Stay put. You're safest to just stay here."

The farm administrators loaded up carts, rounded up cattle, and moved out. In their wake, the army disappeared like morning mist, leaving a handful of soldiers behind with orders to blow up the remaining supplies and equipment. Razhivatka grew eerily quiet. When darkness came, Galina and her mother went to bed, only to be awoken a short time later by the landlady.

"They don't want to blow up the food stores," she said. "They want to leave us something to live on."

Suddenly, the future looked less bleak. Nina and Lily grabbed their pillowcases and ran to the storage depot. They returned with bulging sacks of flour and sugar, eggs, butter, and lard. In return for their kindness, the villagers gave the soldiers clothes to replace their uniforms and wished them Godspeed on their journey home. The young men were gone by the time an advance guard of Germans rolled through the streets on motorcycles. The ss had come to Razhivatka.

Some of the Cossacks welcomed the invaders as liberators, presenting them with bread and salt on embroidered towels. Others were more cautious in their enthusiasm, but everyone saw the fascists as an improvement over the hated Communists. Once the last Soviet bureaucrats had fled, the Cossacks toppled the white clay statue of Stalin that graced the *stanitsa* square, cheering "*Lyubo!*" as it shattered on the ground. One of the smashed arms was turned into a hitching post for goats.

By noon of the following day, the Alpine Division had arrived and hunkered down, awaiting orders to continue their march across the Caucasus to the oilfields of Maikop and Baku. They were friendly and sympathetic, and they warned against the Romanians advancing in their wake, suggesting that anything valuable should be hidden. They didn't exaggerate. The Romanians blew through Razhivatka like a howling wind, stealing everything that wasn't nailed down, including Galina's toothbrush. It would be months before she got another.

The flood of people who had run from the collective began to trickle back, without belongings, wagons, or herds. Their tales of horror left Galina breathless: the road jammed with cattle, carts, and people, a German plane flying low and strafing them with machine guns, the frightened cattle stampeding, crushing the people trying vainly to control them. Nina mentally blessed the major who had advised them to stay, although Razhivatka had little left to recommend it.

Its storehouses were empty, its homes looted, its barns deserted. In one of them, Galina found a sickly calf with a cast in one eye. He looked so pitiful, huddled in a corner by himself, that Galina had no choice but to bring him home. Nina was unimpressed, the landlady even less so. Galina's new pet was as loyal as a dog, but he lacked any social graces. He raided the vegetable garden, left puddles and piles near the doorway, and generally made a nuisance of himself. When Galina went to the outhouse, he missed her and, unable to knock, simply butted down the walls. The latticed sunflower stalks collapsed as completely as the landlady's patience. Reluctantly, Galina returned the calf to his barn.

In the days that followed there were happy reunions with sons, brothers, and husbands who had fled the collapsing front. The Germans recruited many of the Cossacks, initially in small squadrons, later in growing numbers until, in 1943, an entire division was formed. Over their uniforms, Cossacks wore their traditional *burkas*: stiff, heavy, square-shouldered riding cloaks made of camel or goat hair. A wooden yoke underneath created impossibly wide shoulders. There was an air of Slavic romanticism about these men as they stood together, backs poker straight, their lambskin hats at a rakish tilt. Their tunics were cinched with wide belts and their baggy pants tucked into knee-high boots. Closing her eyes, Galina breathed in deeply, and let the smell of leather conjure up a vision of her father.

γ

The weather turned cold. The little parlour in which they slept was unheated and Nina was forced to scout out a hut near the center of the *stanitsa,* hoping its clay oven might provide both a cooking facility and a warm shelf to sleep on. Now that they, too, lived in an occupied zone, Alexei's money had stopped coming. Although they received a share of the season's crop and a load of sunflower stalks for fuel, there was no prospect of work to help them through the long winter ahead. On market day, Nina arranged a ride to the railroad settlement at Alexandrovka, where she sold the few remaining valuables they owned. Lily walked several miles to the salt mines that lay to the southeast and returned with a full backpack and bruised shoulders. Salt was a useful commodity for barter.

November was cold and rainy and the tracks that had been dust all summer turned to mud. People ventured outside only for drinking water. More than once Galina found herself mired in the muck with a pail of water sinking at her side. Evenings were short; an improvised wick in a jar of sunflower oil offered meagre light. They bundled themselves into bed early, letting the heat from the oven seep up into their bones. They passed the long hours reciting poems from memory and playing number games. Come morning they were instantly alert for the first sign of smoke from their neighbours' chimneys. Then one of them would scamper out to get some starter for their own fire. Dried dung made good fuel, but it was difficult to light and needed constant attention to keep it burning.

At the end of the month, the Germans began to recruit civilians to work in their factories.

"Volunteers?" Lily said.

"Of course. Unless their quota isn't met."

"Well?"

Nina shrugged. "What choice do we have, really? At least we'll
be warm and well fed."

The other Leningrad refugees, who faced an equally bleak
future on the collective, also signed on as "volunteers," as did a
number of local girls eager to leave the farm at any price. The other
citizens of Razhivatka were allowed to remain in their homes.

By the time the record-keeping formalities were completed,
the muddy ground was frozen. A strong, cold wind swept bundles
of tumbleweed across the prairie. Nina, Galina, and Lily packed
up their few remaining goods, Lily's precious photos among
them. The ribbon that bound her small treasure was still tied in
the bow she had set in Leningrad, but the ends were beginning
to fray. Like a film winding in reverse, they were shipped back
along the cart track to the station at Alexandrovka and loaded
into cattle cars. The doors slid shut behind them. They were left
freezing in the dark.

The next morning the train rolled into Kropotkin. There it
met unexpected, and unexplained, delay. Its passengers disembarked, confused by the lapse in German efficiency. Neither
provision nor accommodation had been organized and for several days the refugees lived out of a large, empty warehouse,
dependent for food on what they had brought with them. But
they were free to wander in the town. Galina was keen to explore
the marketplace with her friends. In an alley, they chanced on a
blind man telling fortunes and they stopped to listen. Suddenly,
the man reached out and took Galina's hand. Stroking her palm,
he said, "You have a long road ahead of you, daughter. You will go
across oceans and never return to your homeland." Galina was

shaken. She had no money to pay him and no answer to give. When Nina heard of it, she gave her daughter a coin and told her to pay the old man for his trouble. But when Galina returned to the market, the fortune teller had vanished.

From Kropotkin they moved northeast. It wasn't the most direct route to the Reich but partisans had blocked the local rail lines, forcing the Germans to divert their trains to Stalingrad before heading west. Although the Wehrmacht still held the upper hand at Stalingrad, their strength was waning. The desperate Soviets had established a new line of defence and they threw their massed weight against it, determined to make their last stand at the shining city on the Volga.

The train doors that had stood open when they passed through Stalingrad in May were bolted shut in December. Galina took her turn on the shoulders of her fellows to peer out the small, high window at the blackened ruins of the once proud city. The devastation was total. It spread westward across the burned out villages of the Ukraine, all the way to the Polish border.

Somewhere in Poland the train stopped and the Leningraders were disinfected and transferred to passenger trains. Those who couldn't pass medical inspection were forced to stay behind. Families who had clung together through so much were finally parted forever.

It was a shock to Galina to see so many happy, well-dressed people in the train station. Many of them carried colourfully wrapped packages under their arms and they greeted each other with laughter and good wishes for a merry Christmas. The contrast with what she had left behind was almost unbearable.

From *Europe at Work in Germany: Sauckel Mobilizes the Labor Reserves* by Friedrich Didier. Published in Nazi Germany, 1943. Fritz Sauckel was pleni-potentiary for Labor, 1942–1945. He was executed in 1946 by the Nuremburg Tribunal for Crimes Against Humanity.

Europe at Work in Germany
Sauckel Mobilizes the Labour Reserves

*Almost daily, transports from nearly every nation
of Europe bring workers to Germany. Their numbers
grow as the requirements of the army increase and
as more and more German workers exchange their
factory garb for military uniforms. A substantial
percentage have already proven that they can be
of real help in German factories.*

*Millions of workers from nearly every European
nation are working in the German war industry
today. They now repair some of the damage that
their irresponsible leaders caused for Europe's peoples.*

*Three quarters of the foreign workers in Greater
Germany come from formerly enemy nations,
regions that may even yet be incited by unbelievable
propaganda. This poses a danger that we are aware
of, but it also gives us an unprecedented opportunity
to conduct an educational campaign in the middle
of the war. The Reich can show them daily that we
are qualified to be not only Europe's leading military
nation, but also the model of economic, social and
human qualities.*

*Workers from 25 nations are our guests for months
or years. These foreign workers are proof that their
peoples were the victims of the lies of the base and
corrupt criminals of Jewish plutocracy and Bolshevist*

*hangmen. Now they have seen the true Germany with
their own eyes and experienced social and medical
services that no one even dreams of in Soviet Russia.
They have seen how developed Germany is in all
areas, and have found a culture so advanced that they
are not only astonished, but also realize how misled
they were by the enormous decades-long Judeo-
capitalist or Bolshevist propaganda.*

*Each German in these critical years works sacrifi-
cially and accomplishes astonishing things. We must
constantly show that this extreme level of exertion is
the result not of force, but of an inner sense of obliga-
tion, that we are driven by a mission that makes us
shining examples, that we will not rest until the final
victory is won and each foreign worker has joined
us by mastering with us a common task.*

Future generations will thank us.

PLOUGHSHARES INTO SWORDS

Germany, 1942–1945

Galina's family arrived at Ludwigshutte on Christmas day 1942. The factory they would be working in adjoined the railroad station, so they saw nothing of the nearby town of Biedenkopf. A short walkway led from the platform into the fenced courtyard of a stone mansion and its visions of elegant ladies on the arms of bewhiskered gentlemen. The garden had the lifeless, waiting look of winter, blooms faded and petals fallen, but on the factory wall the ivy still flourished, covering the brickwork with green. The words of Galina's geography teacher rang in her ears: "German winters are 'poor orphan' winters." She had meant that German winters were mild. In their threadbare clothes and worn out shoes, Galina thought the Leningraders had become poor orphans. They were ushered past the big house toward the distant building that would be their quarters.

Galina eyed the long room on the second floor with interest. It was lined with two tiers of shelves. She giggled at the idea of needing so much space to store their luggage. Her giggles stopped as soon as she discovered the room was a dormitory and the shelves, beds. Three German women handed out their new uniforms: nightgowns of rough, blue-striped ticking, badly fitted skirts and jackets in muddy green, and wooden clogs.

They filed into a dingy downstairs room where they dined on *kohlrabi* purée, boiled potatoes still in their skins, and herb tea.

Well, Galina thought, as the saying goes, everything looks better in the morning. She only hoped it was true.

The next day, the chief of police arrived from Biedenkopf to lay out the rules. The Leningraders, like all other Russian workers, must wear blue and white badges printed with the letters OST to identify them as Ostarbeiters. They were free to go into the nearby towns and villages, but if they wanted to travel further a special permit would have to be obtained from his office. "You will be paid fairly, according to our German wage scales," he said. "However, since Ostarbeiters workers have been classified as 'auxiliary workers' only, the cost of your room and board will be deducted from your wages. In addition, you must pay the surtax on eastern workers."

Nina and Lily exchanged sour looks. Why not just call them slave labour and be done with it?

Dates and times were arranged by the document centre for official photographs. Passports were confiscated, for safekeeping.

Still, thought Galina, however depressing their current situation, they at least had the advantages of heat, electricity, running water, and a proper toilet. And — the plum in the pudding — they would be allowed to use the factory shower room once a week.

Meanwhile, the factory itself remained as much of an enigma as the collective farm had been. Galina spent a restless night wondering what lay in store on the other side of the Buderuswerke sign.

"*Aufstehen,* comrades!" The night watchman banged on the door. The inmates hastily rose, dressed, and gathered in the dining room where a group of factory foremen stood waiting to select workers for their departments. Nina and Lily went to the sawmill, Galina to the kitchen.

She was overwhelmed by its size. From the sparkling kettles on the fire to the shining spoons hanging on the wall, everything in the room was massive. A long table dwarfed the two teenaged girls who sat at one end of it, industriously peeling carrots. The girls smiled shyly at Galina, then handed her a pot and a knife and pointed to a huge stack of the vegetables waiting to be cut. Galina's mind flew to Razhivatka and the ignominy of "not everything green is a weed." Would she never escape the curse of the pesky carrot?

ii

An overcrowded train rattled slowly northwest toward Berlin. In it, a thousand Serbs bound for the labour camps of the Reich sat two to a seat or crouched in the aisles. Dragan was among them. He had been arrested when Wehrmacht soldiers made one of their regular sweeps through the streets of Belgrade, rounding up anyone able-bodied enough to work. The sack of potatoes Dragan carried offered no defence against the Luger waved in his face. His capture was all the more humiliating for being uncontested. He counted it a personal failure that he had been caught at all.

Yugoslavia lay in Dragan's past and the last images he had of it left him choking back bile: whole towns where the destruction wrought by the Germans and the Ustashi had left the inhabitants nothing to fight over or to liberate. A magician's hand might have stopped all life in them. Every house had been razed to the ground, leaving nothing but rusted nails, scorched grass, and weeds. There was no trace of human beings.

Horror stories were legion. Women and children, old men and their wives uprooted and whipsawed in the never-ending warfare between the guerrillas and the occupation forces. Burned out of their homes and villages by marauding troops, civilians flooded the countryside, blindly fleeing their oppressors to avoid being shot or sent to concentration camps. The refugees' goal, which shifted constantly with the tide of battle, was some remote region that reportedly had been liberated by the guerrillas. Along the way, thousands died of starvation, exhaustion, or disease. The ragged remnants, inured to pain and hardship, marched grimly on, and only the children whimpered, like small puppies that had lost their mothers.

The train lurched across a stretch of uneven track and the men perched in the aisle toppled over each other like dominoes. Armed guards with secure handholds watched dispassionately as others were thrown from their seats. Dragan's head struck the window support beside him.

"Fuck!"

His seatmate grimaced as he scratched his chest. "I'll be drawing blood soon, I'm so covered with their damned fumigating powder. Christ, it makes me itch!"

A beat of silence and the two burst into laughter.

"Talk about adding insult to injury," Dragan said. "Fritz could shoot us any time and here we are complaining about bug spray and goose eggs." He put out a hand. "Dragan Metikos."

"Petar Krasova. D'you have any idea where they're taking us?"

"I heard Berlin."

Petar whistled. "The heart of the Fatherland. It'll be tough to get out of there."

Dragan raised an eyebrow.

"Well, we have to try to escape, don't we?" Petar said.

Dragan shrugged to ease the sudden tension in his shoulders. "It's not our duty to escape."

"It sure as hell isn't our duty to work for the bastards," Petar said. "Don't tell me you're one of those willing to play along."

Dragan flexed his hands. "I'm not a soldier on a mission," he said, "just a fellow trying to hang on 'til the war is over. Maybe by then we'll be able to figure out who the good guys are. If there are any."

Petar said, "You're not an advocate of dying in the attempt?"

"I'm attempting to survive. Dying would be counterproductive."

"Is that how you see survival? As a job to be done, a task to be accomplished?"

"Yes."

"So you don't think about anything except how to do that."

"No."

"You try very hard not to feel anything?"

"Yes."

Petar frowned. "But you're bound to feel something. You are human."

"Hold that thought," Dragan said.

Petar stared at him, then shrugged and said, "What do you suppose we'll be doing for Fritz meantime?"

Dragan shrugged. "Building air raid shelters, digging coal."

"What makes you think so?"

"I overheard the guards."

"You speak German?"

"Some. I learned it at school."

"So what was that they were saying when we got on the train? They seemed to think it was pretty funny."

"They were saying, *'Slav arbeit ist sklave arbeit.'* It means Slav labour is slave labour."

iii

Frau Koppe was in charge of the factory kitchen and the cafeteria; she saw to it that her new charge learned every aspect of her job and at least some of the language. Within a week, Galina could understand what she was being told; within a month she could carry on a conversation. She was careful who she practiced on. Not everyone was as sympathetic as Frau Koppe, and for every German who felt sorry for the prisoners and slipped them extra crusts of bread, there were others who treated them with open contempt. Even this cloud had its silver lining. The officers who occupied the mansion when the labourers arrived soon decided they didn't want to share the courtyard with foreigners. They moved on, leaving space in the beautiful house for the despised aliens. It was a return toward the nearly forgotten luxuries of privacy and comfort. Instead of a dormitory or a small hut, five women now shared two large rooms. True, the furnishings were sparse: a few stools and a bench on either side of a long table and five beds in one room, a wardrobe and closet in the other. Nina improvised a dressing table by placing an empty suitcase on top of one of the stools and covering it in a sheet. Her small touch of elegance was a compliment to the parquet floors, the papered walls, and the draped windows that overlooked the garden and the creek.

Galina woke on the morning of April 20 to find a small jeweller's box beside her pillow. Nestled inside was a delicate silver necklace. She felt like a princess when she fastened it round her neck. She hadn't expected anything beyond good wishes, but Nina had produced a special present for her daughter's sixteenth birthday. Who had managed the purchase and where had the money come from? Galina wondered. Her mother's takehome pay barely covered the cost of the precious, black market cigarettes she acquired through Reinhardt, the factory chauffeur.

It seemed that all of Ludwigshutte was celebrating that day. Nazi flags fluttered at the train station, the factory, and the shops. Banners of red and black festooned the houses. The mill workers asked Nina if she knew what the occasion was. "Of course," Nina answered straight-faced. "It's my daughter's birthday." Her coworkers were aghast and launched into earnest explanation that it was the *Fuhrer's* birthday that mattered. Nina listened gravely, wondering how a nation that so passionately espoused "strength through joy" could be so completely humourless.

The former occupants hadn't bothered to sweep up when they left the mansion. The rooms, stairs, and large hall needed to be thoroughly cleaned and the floors washed. To Galina's eyes it was a daunting and disagreeable task. But here the farm girls from Razhivatka who had previously kept their distance came in handy. With no future at all on the *stanitsa,* they had been among the first to volunteer for work in Germany. So far they hadn't been disappointed. They had eagerly embraced "city life": they enjoyed the effect the permanent waves in their hair and the high heels on their feet had on the Russian, Ukrainian, and Polish boys who laboured on nearby farms. Now they wanted to learn to dance like ladies. Galina became their teacher. It wasn't the Kirov Ballet, but it was better than scrubbing floors. In exchange for showing them the intricacies of the foxtrot and the waltz, Galina's students did her share of the cleaning. She considered it a fair trade. It wasn't so easy humming a tune while guiding plump, clumsy bodies around the floor. Once word of the lessons got out, Galina had no problem with housekeeping.

The problem of food required more effort. The factory supplied one hot meal a day — vegetarian, fat-free — and a small ration of bread, margarine, and sugar measured in granules, once a week. In Germany, as in Razhivatka and the rest of Europe, all able-bodied men were serving at the front. Farmers forced to split their time between work at the factory and work on the farm were always eager to find extra hands for the field and more than willing to pay for them in kind. Nina and Lily jumped at the chance to supplement their food ration. So did the strong farm girls of Razhivatka, who were always in great demand and the first to be chosen for any job. Galina's efforts took a more artistic turn. Using scraps of plywood from the wood shop where she built crates for ammunition, Nina cut simple kewpie dolls. Galina painted on rosy cheeks and Cupid's bow lips and sold the finished dolls to local shops.

Summer arrived and the woods surrounding Ludwigshutte grew lush with strawberries, raspberries, and mushrooms, which disappeared as quickly as they ripened. Galina was summoned from the kitchen to the factory director's villa on the hill overlooking the train station. She never learned who had recommended her for the post, but the director's wife wanted a holiday companion for her granddaughter. Galina's refined air suited her better than the earthier disposition of the other girls. She was provided with a bicycle and a knitted woollen bathing suit. The summer of 1943 became for Galina an interlude of roaming the countryside and swimming in the river Lahn. In the fall she returned to the factory.

iv

Once the first bludgeoning shock of capture had passed, uncertainty and fear persisted. In the days between his arrest and his deportation from Belgrade, Dragan had felt he might go mad. His mind was tortured over the question of when, or whether, he would be free again. Rounds of interrogation by scornful German officers had added to the indignities of imprisonment. There were long hours of forced inactivity when there was nothing to fill his mind but unfocussed guilt. He should have tried harder to escape, he should have joined the Partisans, he should have fought back, not run from Petrinja. But what about reprisals, an inner voice had mocked. Is your life worth a hundred others? In his saner moments, Dragan knew the answer was still no, though that had been easier to believe in Belgrade, where he had managed to fashion a life for himself in spite of his circumstances.

The humiliation of being caught had been sickening. What was worse, Dragan learned, was the instinctive need of the victim to be well thought of by his captors. The reflex to self-preservation impelled him to do his best even as a slave, but he tried to keep his mind blank while he did it. If you weren't careful, he found, you started thinking of things. And if you thought of things, you went crazy.

For Dragan, journey's end had been the Berlin suburb of Nicholassee, where workers were sorted and shunted to jobs.

"Based on what?" Petar said. "The number of moles on my back? I swear if they give me one more physical exam I won't just feel like a lab rat, I'll turn into one. How good does a guy have to look to dig coal in the Ruhrgebiet?"

"I don't think they really care about your baby blue eyes," Dragan said.

"No? And how about that silver tongue of yours? How far did your Sunday school German get you?"

Dragan grinned. "Into a truck instead of a mine, my friend."

"A truck? What do you know about trucks? You've probably never even sat in one."

"True. But I'll be sitting in one now and the Germans are going to teach me how to drive it."

"Lucky bastard."

Berlin had become a forest of barracks where every open space, large or small, was home to another pinewood and tar-paper dormitory. The city resembled a vast encampment with a garrison woven around heroic monuments, office buildings, train stations, and factories. Berlin was no longer just the capital city of the Third Reich; it had become the country's single most important armoury. One in ten airplane motors, one in four tanks, and fully half the guns produced in Germany in 1943 were produced in Berlin. Nearly half a million slave labourers and prisoners of war — men and women — worked in the streets and factories of the city.

The truck driver training centre was a Tower of Babel dominated by Russian POWs eager to trade the hunger and misery of the camps for the comparative comforts of Berlin, and their striped ticking prison garb for old French army uniforms dyed black. Mechanical theory was taught in the morning by two Russian émigrés who had become French citizens after the first war and German prisoners in the second. Officers of the Reich who had been wounded in battle and invalided home put the trainees through their paces behind the wheel in the afternoon.

Dragan practiced shifting gears and manoeuvring loads through city streets that were at times barely passable. While workers strained to clear the rubble left by British bombers, the Americans emptied more payloads.

"I just hope they don't land one of those things on us by mistake."

Dragan nodded. He and a fellow Serb, Dusan, were changing the oil on a truck under the watchful eye of a soldier with a shock of blonde hair and a peach complexion.

"Do you figure he shaves yet?" said Dusan.

"Doubt it. They're getting younger all the time. Practically everyone over eighteen has already been sent to the front."

"Which sounds like it's getting closer every day."

The young guard moved a few paces toward them and stopped a cautious five feet away. The gun he held looked too heavy for his hand. Dragan wondered if he knew how to fire it.

The boy spoke in a surprising baritone.

"You men must be silent. There is to be no conversation. Do you understand?"

Dragan and Dusan stared at him.

"Silence. Yes?" The boy's voice betrayed him on the yes, slipping into a falsetto that made him flush with embarrassment.

"We could take him easily," Dusan said.

"Sure," Dragan said. "And then what? We're in Berlin. Talk about a rock and a hard place, we've got the Germans on the ground and the Allies in the air." He screwed the oil cap back in place and wiped his hands on a rag. "Here comes my instructor. I'm supposed to practice night driving tonight."

"Well, watch your back," Dusan said. "It's the Brits' favourite time of day."

The truck's headlights glinted on dust motes that hung like a gossamer shroud over the remains of shattered buildings and ruptured cobbles. Dragan drove easily now, his pleasure in this newfound skill unspoiled by the rigid figure beside him.

Major Bauer had no visible injury, but his face bore the lines and pallor of the chronically ill. From time to time, a spasm of pain twisted his mouth. The Major spoke only to give directions. Dragan enjoyed the silence. Secure in this little metal box, he felt he could drive forever. He had only to point the vehicle southeast and it would take him back to Belgrade and the familiar sights and sounds of home. He fantasized that the war was over, the Germans and Ustashi no longer held sway over the Serbs, and he was free to design his own heaven on earth.

The scream of an air raid siren jolted him out of his reverie.

"Kill the lights. And pull over there."

Dragan parked the truck neatly by the curb. It occurred to him that precision could hardly matter this time; if a bomb landed on the corner, the truck would be history.

"Out," said Major Bauer. He didn't bother to unholster his pistol.

Planes blotted out the stars. Streets deserted a moment before were suddenly alive with people scurrying to find shelter underground.

Major Bauer shook his head. "Not for us," he said. "There will be no room." He pointed. "Over there."

"Over there" was a bomb crater, perhaps thirty feet wide. To Dragan it didn't seem to offer much protection. He glanced at Bauer's face and realized that the Major didn't care. Dragan did. He quite liked the idea of living to see another day.

The first bombs fell miles away, while the two men were still climbing over the edge of the crater. Its roughly terraced walls reminded Dragan of Ivo and the neat row they had hoed together before Dragan slipped into the woods and began his hike to Blinjski Kut.

Major Bauer sat with his back against the crater wall, took out a cigarette and lit it. Dragan dug himself a toehold that allowed him to peer out over the top of the makeshift shelter and watch the oncoming juggernaut. The planes advanced in waves, edging closer as inexorably as the tide into Mrtvo More, a lifetime ago on the island of Lokrum.

The ground shuddered and a bomb blast hammered Dragan. He dropped back below the rim of the crater with his hands over his ears and began to pray.

He didn't know how long he stayed there, curled up like a fetus in the dirt. Eventually, the trembling earth steadied and the roaring died away as the last of the bombers disappeared into the distance. Major Bauer had not shifted his position. He still held a cigarette to his lips. For a moment, Dragan wondered if it was the same one he had lit when the first bomb fell. Then he noticed the small pile of butts in the dirt.

"You'd better take a look," the Major said, "but I suspect we'll be walking."

Dragan crawled to the edge of the crater and peered out at the city.

Berlin was a landscape of black and orange where smoke and flame twisted wildly across the facades of broken buildings. Even the dust motes flickered. Dragan covered his mouth and nose with his sleeve, and with his free hand, brushed scorching particles from his hair. A block away, the side street where he had parked the truck was a tunnel of fire, the truck itself a blazing pillar at its mouth. Over the roar of the inferno, he could hear the screams of people trapped in the conflagration.

A figure staggered out onto the street, engulfed in flame.

Automatically Dragan reached out a hand and leaned forward, but the gesture was only a reflex. The blackening shape was too far away to help and it was already crumbling to the pavement.

Dragan shrank back into the makeshift bunker, as sweaty and weak as a man suffering from ague. He looked at Major Bauer, but the Major continued to stare straight ahead. His face held no expression at all.

Two days later, the commandant announced that a dozen of the training camp inmates would be moving west. The Ruhrgebiet, thought Dragan. I guess I'll be joining Dusan in the mines after all.

γ

By the time her "companion summer" ended, Galina's old position in the kitchen had been filled by one of the thousands of Germans fleeing the Allied bombardment of their cities. She was assigned a new task: to inspect and repair imperfections in the moulds for small bombs. She wondered if, two years ago, someone like her had cast the bombs that fell on Leningrad. She thought about the unexploded bomb she and Lidya had found and wondered at the irony of it.

At the end of the first day, with no tools or protective gloves, Galina's fingers were raw and bleeding from the sandy compound used to smooth out the mould. Once its surface was even, a mould was set into a form to be cast and here the terrifying part of the job began. Heat slapped Galina's face as soon as she stepped through the door of the foundry. The blast furnace looked like a living thing vomiting flames. Labourers black with sweat and ash fed scrap iron into the monstrous oven and tapped molten metal from its crucible. Bubbles of vapour danced across its surface as though tossed by invisible hands in some kind of rhythmic sport. A constant roar issued from its gaping mouth.

Galina was happy when she was transferred to the shop where her friend Genrietta worked. A cool, reserved blonde, Genya had ridden the same train from Leningrad and hoed the same carrot patch in Razhivatka. Now she and Galina spent the days together assembling small heating stoves for the Germans.

A group of young Frenchmen was delivered to work at the factory, looking as bewildered and confused as the Ostarbeiters had when they first arrived. Most had never seen a factory before, let alone worked in one, but they were so charming and well-mannered that the old hands were pleased to take them under their wing. Romance flourished, aided by Saturday evening dances. Tables in the common dining room were pushed aside and the young people twirled to the music of a mouth organ, when they were lucky, and a comb and tissue paper when they were not. At 10:30 the lights flickered a warning. At 11:00 the gates were locked and the Frenchmen, who were housed across the river by the sawmill, had to be back in their own quarters. One of the young men was a talented pianist. With the blessing of the factory administrator, a Christmas concert was arranged and a semi-tuned piano moved to the dining room for the occasion. The repertoire was vetted in advance but to Galina, deprived of her beloved Tchaikovsky for so long, even the German composers sounded heavenly. It was the young pianist's last performance. A few days after the concert he had an accident in the mill and lost the fingers of his right hand to an electric saw. A month later, Nina suffered a similar accident, but she was luckier: the blades only sliced through the tips of her fingers and didn't cut the bone. The dangling pieces of flesh were sewn back in place. The mill workers were accustomed to accidents; the saws had protective guards but they were awkward and seldom used.

Constant mending notwithstanding, the Leningraders' clothes and shoes were falling apart. In spite of the unhealthy diet, Galina grew out of her dresses. Nina took apart the cotton comforter on her bed and Mrs. Pumponen, one of the Finnish labourers, made two dresses from it: a beige one from the lining and a paisley print from the cover. Galina traded some of her kewpie dolls for a pair of smart red sandals with wooden soles and was happy with result. The shoes reminded her of the prized pair Nina had bought her so long ago.

Shortly after they arrived at Ludwigshutte the workers were marched into the courtyard and told they could select one pair of shoes each from the supply that had just been delivered by truck. It was a motley assortment of men's, women's, and children's footwear that ran the gamut from boots to high-heeled slippers. Some were quite scuffed; others well-kept. None were new. The labourers stared, afraid to ask where the shoes had come from. They had heard whispers about special camps and the people in them who, apparently, had no more need of shoes. It did no good to wonder why or to speculate on how long it might be before they, too, no longer needed shoes. Galina asked Petry, the factory cobbler, to mend hers yet again. "Just make them last til the end of the war," she said. He smiled sourly at her little joke.

Everyone continued to supplement the camp diet with berries and mushrooms from the nearby woods. Foraging had become as much an entertainment as a necessity. Galina and Genya took a different path through the trees every day looking for untapped sources of food.

"What's that over there?" Genya said. She pointed to what looked like a giant white mushroom in the bracken. They approached it cautiously, wary of possible danger. Sensing none, they dropped to their knees beside their find.

"Mmm, silk," Galina said. She ran appreciative fingers over the fine, sleek fabric and rubbed a fistful of it against her cheek. "It's a parachute."

There was no way to tell how the chute had come to be there — no sign either that an injured airman had dragged himself away or that someone had landed in the clearing on purpose and stuffed it out of sight under the ferns. Plane engines were a common sound in the skies over Ludwigshutte and daily becoming more so. According to the French boys, the English and the Americans were now targeting Kassel to the northeast. At intervals, the factory siren shrilled, ordering everyone into the air raid shelter that had been dug into the side of the hill on the other side of the creek. Galina and Genya didn't take the alarm seriously. They seized the opportunity to stop work and sneak away to lie in the tall grass, where they could gossip undetected and watch the sky for the first sight of heavily loaded Allied planes.

As autumn waned and no bombs fell on Ludwigshutte, they grew bolder in their defiance and, tired of the grass, made for the factory roof, which provided a fine, flat surface for tanning under the dwindling rays of the sun. Inevitably, they were spotted by the guard they hated most: a belligerent Nazi who levelled his gun at them and screamed, *"Achtung! Aufstehen, die beide Madchen da! Kommen sie sofort runter!"* He denounced the girls as enemies of the Reich, claiming they had gained access to the roof in order to signal to the enemy flying high overhead. He could have shot them out of hand, but fate intervened in the form of a sympathetic captain who sentenced them to garbage duty instead of death.

Galina wondered what the Nazi guard would have to say if he caught them with the parachute. She and Genya looked at each other.

"Finders keepers?" Galina suggested. Genya nodded.

They folded the bulging material until it could be reasonably, if clumsily, concealed under Galina's dress. "I look like a good German hausfrau now, don't I?"

"Well, if anyone tries to hug you, they'll certainly wonder what you're made of."

Praying no one would notice them, the girls made their way quietly back to the house, where they cut the parachute into pieces that later became fine silk blouses.

More newcomers, a small group of sad-faced men in Italian uniform, were added to the ranks of workers in the factory. They had been party to the Badoglio rebellion that deposed Mussolini and sued for peace with the Allies; they were traitors to the Axis cause. The German forces who restored the Duce to power, however briefly, had reacted to the setback with predictable ferocity, executing many of the rebels and shipping the remainder to labour camps.

As the aerial attacks on Germany continued, its citizens fled their homes in increasing numbers. The trickle of refugees pushing carts and baby carriages laden with their worldly goods was swelling to a stream. German strength was beginning to fail and the slaves at Ludwigshutte sensed it. But the local workers at the sawmill continued their show of bravado, pointing to the map on the wall still covered in the coloured pins of German domination. "Look," they said proudly, "look, it's all ours."

Nina replied, "The war isn't over yet."

vi

As the war ground on, the Reich transported an endless stream of foreign workers into its crippled heartland in a desperate effort to repair the damage inflicted on its mines and factories, its railway lines, and waterworks. Labour camps multiplied throughout the Ruhrgebiet. Their inmates toiled alongside the local villagers, and died with them under walls of water when British bombers destroyed the dams that held back the Ruhr.

Dragan wasn't sent to the coalmines. He was assigned instead as assistant to another slave, a Polish driver hauling endless loads of gravel to the site of the shattered Mohne dam. The breach in the dam had loosed floods that drowned camps and factories for forty miles downstream. Flying home from their mission, retreating Allied bombers had dropped incendiaries onto upstream barges all the way along the river. Dragan thought that, from the sky, they must have looked like Viking funeral pyres.

He could imagine the terror of the barge workers. He could understand the gratification the pilots must have felt. But his throat ached and his shoulders tightened when he thought about the slaves. How many thousands had there been? Faceless, nameless victims yanked from their homelands, yoked to the German war machine and swept away by the deluge. Their numbers would never appear in official reports.

After a few months at the dam site, Dragan was handed on to a construction crew at Essen-Werden. In peacetime the town had been a spa where members of the upper crust and high-level bureaucrats could relax beside the waters of the Baldeneysee and admire the flowers in Gruga Park. In wartime it had become a retreat for German commanders on the western front. Beribboned officers hunkered down at the Krupp family's Villa Hugel, a palace surrounded by a mini-forest and lush green lawns. Dragan's job was to help build a bunker in the hillside below it.

For days on end his ears rang with the clatter of a jackhammer and his arm muscles twitched uncontrollably. But he counted himself lucky. The generals and their aides enjoyed the best of everything and those who worked for them became accidental beneficiaries. Dragan was housed in decent barracks — nothing unsightly to spoil the generals' view — and he was well fed. He even had Sundays off to wander the neighbourhood and take a girl to the movies. It was ironic, he thought, that the Germans insisted on maintaining some semblance of a labour code and on

paying out monthly wages, however small, as though compensa-
tion could redeem a worker's slave status. Or the euphemistic
label "foreign worker" make him free.

Inherent in the German plan for world conquest was the
systematic subjugation of "racially inferior" eastern Europeans,
whose labour became one of the perquisites of racial annihi-
lation. Between the extremes of being doomed to death as a
slave and living a normal life as an itinerant worker, were many
shades of grey. Special decrees left the Ostarbeiters defenceless
against arbitrary persecution by the Gestapo and other police
services. Like all foreigners in Germany, they were closely
watched by a bureaucratic and racist control apparatus composed of the Wehrmacht, the Arbeitsamt, the Werkschutz, the
SS, and the Gestapo.

The ersatz normalcy of earnings and taxes could not disguise
the fact that forced labourers lived only as long they were useful
to the Reich. They were captives, forcibly removed from their
homelands, deprived of free will, dependent on their enemy for
food. Dragan found grim satisfaction in counting the number of
German troops required to watch their prisoners eat.

On a cold night in December 1944, when the generals were
safely tucked inside their newly dug bunker, a stray bomb landed
near Werden, but it did no real damage. The brunt of the Allied
attack was aimed at what remained of the coalmines and factories of Essen. Wrapped in a thinning blanket and perched on a
rock outside the bunker, Dragan saw British bombers advancing
from the northwest in the same implacable waves he had seen in
Berlin. He watched them release their devastating payloads on
the thousand years of history below. He had ignored the air raid
siren, preferring to take his chances outside rather than join the
crowd cowering underground.

From a distance of fifteen miles, the raid had the surreal
quality of a massive fireworks display. Though it was much too

far away for Dragan to hear the screams of fear and pain on the streets of the city, the roar of engines and the crash of exploding firebombs carried clearly on the night air. From the hillside at Werden the landscape looked like a giant playing field on which the enormity of war had been reduced to a game of strategy, with each side trying to position its pieces for maximum gain. In a game, Dragan thought, contestants play to win but they play without threat to themselves. In real life, nations play to win, and human beings become just another resource to be managed while armies struggle to protect and advance their positions. In real life, when pieces are moved and power plays are set in motion, real people suffer. And real people die.

Dragan drew up his knees and wrapped his arms around himself in a futile effort to feel warm.

vii

Christmas came and went at the BuderusWerke in an atmosphere that was anything but festive. Food rations were dwindling and no one was working on the farms. Nearly every house in Biedenkopf and the surrounding villages sheltered German families fleeing Allied bombs. The teenagers who had recently taken Galina and Genya sledding on the hills behind the factory now proudly wore the black uniform of the Abwehr, Germany's Home Guard. A collection of adolescents and old men. Whispers and rumour swirled through the factory. The main road was clogged with refugees, some heading east, others west, all targets for low flying planes. The dining room in the mansion became a makeshift hospital for the wounded, with mattresses spread on the floor and the local doctor doing what he could to patch people up and send them on their way.

In March the factory stopped production, the farmers stayed in their villages, and a new rumour began to circulate: the guards had orders to eliminate all foreigners before the Allies arrived. Word went round that the Americans were only a few days from Biedenkopf; the Ostarbeiters decided to play it safe. The German guards had disappeared from the courtyard and the gates were no longer locked. Unsure of what was happening, the Leningraders waited for darkness and then headed for the hills, planning to stay hidden until the American army arrived.

The weather didn't cooperate. For two days they huddled miserably in the woods, shivering under the constant drizzle. On the third day, scouts returned with the happy news that the Americans were nearly there, and the bedraggled workers came out from behind the trees and rushed down the hill to greet them. The more level-headed made for the safety of a building, but Galina and her friends beelined for the centre of town to cheer on the tanks that were rolling down the street. Their turrets stood open. The American soldiers inside grinned and waved at the crowd of people shouting approval and waving white flags they had ripped from sheets or shirts or whatever else lay handy. Galina was a little nonplussed by her liberators. Why did so many of them look like cows chewing at their cuds?

Before she had the chance to find out, or to sample some gum for herself, sniper fire erupted from the hills. With the speed of long practice, turret covers slammed shut and the Americans began to return fire. The people in the street scrambled for cover. Galina turned to run, stumbled, and nearly fell as the heel broke off one of her shoes. A strong arm grabbed her by the elbow and hustled her toward the river. Galina fought down a crazy desire to laugh. She had asked Petry to mend her shoes well enough to last to the end of the war and he had timed it to the minute.

"Far enough, I think. We should be safe here."

Galina looked at the man who had rescued her from the mayhem in the street and was pleased to see it was Emil, the young

Frenchman who had always been so attentive at the Saturday dances and whose company had warmed Galina during the damp, chilly sojourn in the woods. She took a couple of limping steps and grabbed his arm again. Balancing on her right foot, she pulled the undamaged shoe from her left and wrenched the heel from it.

"Now at least I can walk on an even keel," she said. "Oh!" Emil followed her gaze.

The crocuses and violets that bloomed on the riverbank framed a body that lay crumpled amid them. The medals and insignia on the grey uniform were those of a German captain; his pistol was still in his hand. Galina stared at the man's face. She could understand the despair he must have felt watching his world collapse around him. She wondered if it had been courage or cowardice that drove him to commit suicide to escape it. Emil wrested the gun from the dead man's fingers, then unhooked the ss dagger from the man's belt and handed it to Galina.

"Better safe than sorry," he said.

She weighed the weapon in her palm, feeling its heft. She slid it from its silver sheath to test the sharpness of the blade. "Better safe than sorry," she echoed.

viii

Shortly before Christmas, Dragan had been moved yet again, this time to Selbeck, where he divided his efforts between driving and, because trucks were getting scarcer all the time, a carpenter's shop. He was pleased when he thought of all the time, paperwork, and manpower he had cost the Germans so far. True, he owed more to good luck than good management, but he and millions of slaves like him were keeping whole battalions of Germans from joining their countrymen at the front. He had lost track of the number of jobs he had had since fleeing Petrinja, but their variety had suggested a motto: "If you're stupid with your hands, you may survive the autumn—but you'll never last the winter."

"Do you know anything at all about woodwork?" Carpenter Ivan Milesic regarded his new associate sourly. At least Dragan came from a farm, so there was a chance he could hammer in a nail without taking out his thumb. Not that it really mattered. What they were building didn't require much skill. The workshop they used was in the village; its owner had died defending ten feet of mud in Holland. His tools, which had once fashioned elegant cabinets and dining tables, now built shipping boxes for arms.

Dragan found mild if unexpected satisfaction in creating something from nothing. The agreeable crunch as the saw took its first bite of wood, the pungent smell of the dust that filtered from the cut, the pleasure of seeing shaped boards fit together like pieces of a puzzle, made his new circumstances tolerable.

By the beginning of April 1945, the British army had reached the Rhine. Some of their shells had already landed in Selbeck, collapsing the roofs and walls of several of the houses.

"We're too close to the damn Krupp factory, that's the problem," Dragan said. "They're trying to knock out whatever German industry they can as they advance."

"They're going to advance right into our workshop pretty soon," Ivan said. "And I'd like to get the hell out of the line of fire before they do. D'you think if we tied white rags to our heads and swam across the river, they'd get the message and let us surrender?" He hammered a final nail into the shallow container he was assembling but, instead of adding this one to the stack of boxes waiting for delivery to the Krupp factory, he nudged it along to the other end of the workbench.

Dragan measured it with his eye. "I think it's going to take the Allies months just to sort out what all the armbands and ID patches mean, never mind adding headgear." He sawed a piece of plywood in two. "You ever notice that we're just about the only ones here without IDs? Everyone else has one. 'P' for Pole, 'T' for Tschech, 'O' for Ost. I can't decide which is more humiliating—being tagged like an animal or being considered too lowly a specimen even for that." He picked up a hammer and drove in a series of nails with such force that the indent of the hammerhead was clearly visible around each one.

"The Nazis do have their own view of the world, warped as it is. That's why they hate the Communists so much, you know—they couldn't exist in a society where everyone's equal."

"They're not going to exist in this one much longer either. The western front is moving further east every day and judging by the mood around here, Fritz is rapidly losing interest in his own war."

Ivan slid a second briefcase-sized container along the bench and watched as Dragan drilled pilot holes for hinges and affixed a small wooden handle. There was a footstep on the gravel outside the door and the two men whisked their work out of sight behind the stacks of lumber waiting to become gun boxes. A guard wandered in, glanced around the interior of the shop, and nodded at the stack of boxes standing beside the door.

"These are ready?"

"Yes, sir."

"I'll send someone to pick them up."

The guard left.

Dragan let out a breath. "*Phuh.* I wouldn't want to go through that too many times a day," he said, "even if Fritz is tired of the job. We'd better finish these suitcases and get them out of here. With any luck at all, we should be able to smuggle them into the barracks and under our mattresses."

"They'd actually be an improvement on the pillows."

Dragan laughed. "Maybe we should pilfer a little sawdust along with the plywood."

"Speaking of theft," Ivan said, "I got hold of a bike. And a wagon. I hid them behind the far barrack."

"We'd better get out of here soon, then," Dragan said. "Those are things somebody's going to miss."

Ivan nodded. "If we can get across that back field, we can reach the road. And if we can reach the road ..."

"We can reach the Allies," Dragan said.

The door banged open again and another guard poked his head inside. "Dinner," he said. He left the door standing open as he rejoined the straggly row of labourers being herded back to the barracks for the evening. Dragan tucked one of the homemade suitcases under his jacket. His left arm stuck out at an awkward angle from his side so that his hand could cup the edge of the box, but he didn't think anyone would notice. The jacket hung loosely on his slight frame and the chilly fog that had blanketed Selbeck that morning had turned to cold drizzle by afternoon. The guards kept their collars up and their cap brims down as they hustled their miserable charges along. Nobody seemed to notice when the two men at the back of the line slipped through the door at one end of the barracks and rejoined them at the other.

The whistle and explosive crump of artillery shells rattled the tin plates on the table even as the camp siren blared out a warning. Men paused with bowls halfway to their mouths; others seized the chance to cram more than their share of bread into their pockets. Soldiers straightened their relaxed positions by the doors, anticipating orders from a commandant who didn't appear.

"That was a bit too close for comfort," Ivan said. "It sounded right next door."

"Out!" one of the guards suddenly yelled. "Everybody out!" A moment later, the lights failed and the orderly evacuation of the dining barrack became a confusion of overturned benches and grunts of effort as the prisoners struggled to be first out of a door they could no longer see. Dragan collided heavily with the wall as men shouldered their way past him.

Outside, rain and swirling mist created an impressionist tableau as guards and inmates each tried to decide which way to run for safety. Another explosion shook the ground and sent them scurrying like ants in all directions. The guards seemed bewildered. Should they mount a counterattack? Move their charges to safety? While the guards debated, Dragan and Ivan acted.

In minutes they had liberated their suitcases from the sleeping barrack and thrown their few belongings inside: each had one change of clothes, a thin blanket, and a threadbare towel. Their official documents were always in their pockets. No one moved, even within the camp, without proper identification or the precious Deutschmarks they had been paid. Dragan touched the small pocket over his heart, reassured by the faint rustle of folded paper. Still carefully pressed inside it was the four-leaf clover he had picked the day he left Petrinja.

Dragan's stomach was tight as they pushed their stolen bicycle through the stubble of last year's wheat field. Every so often, Dragan checked the hitch. It would be galling to lose all they owned in the mud because of a loose connection. By the time they reached the road, they had altered their plans for approaching the Allies. With the army moving so quickly and shooting so indiscriminately, they reckoned their chances were better if they tracked east for a while.

In spite of the cold and the wet, they kept a steady pace, staying close to the verge so that, if need be, they could dive for cover into the ditch or escape pursuit in the trees beyond it. Occasionally, they passed a farmhouse nestled in fields slowly waking to spring, or a cluster of a dozen half-timbered houses around a square, but there were no suspicious glances cast their way, no shouts of "Halt," no warning shots fired over their heads.

They plodded on, pushing the bicycle and the wagon between them. Night descended like a shade pulled down over a window. The *crump* of artillery fire dwindled in the distance and the twittering of birds disappeared, leaving only the uneasy stirring of branches and the anxious rustling of boughs overhead.

As the darkness thickened, the trees on either side of the road thinned, opening to fields that looked unpleasantly exposed. The runaways decided to press on. The more distance they could put between themselves and Selbeck, the better. In a way, Dragan thought, escape was like diving off the rock into Mrtvo More, a hopeful leap into the unknown.

The road sloped gently into a broad, shallow valley. Dragan and Ivan moved confidently ahead, their eyes grown accustomed to the shapes and shadows in the darkness. As they passed a house half hidden behind a clump of pines, a dog barked, and dull yellow light filled one of the windows as a lamp was lit. Dragan stared. The glow reached out into the unfriendly dark and held him. It had appeared so quickly, as if someone was lying awake inside the house, listening, waiting. Maybe it was a woman, hoping against hope that her lover or her son was coming home. Maybe chance would smile on her, one never knew.

It seemed to Dragan that the world was composed now of nothing but chance. It had allowed him to survive arrest, bombing, and forced labour, and now it had brought him to this small light in the darkness. He had learned that one chance could lead to another and he was determined to continue making the most of each, in order to preserve himself. Even if the future held no promise of being any better than the past, it was his future, and it was all he had.

They pushed on past the house and the barking dog, until cold and weariness forced them to stop under a tree. There was a tangle of bushes behind it and a screen of bracken in front. Although the curling fronds of bright green fern were not yet fully open, they offered a modicum of safety and there was little likelihood of anyone stumbling across the two men asleep on the cold, damp ground beside a rusty bicycle.

They avoided the larger centre of Essen and Wuppertal in favour of more friendly villages where they could find food and shelter, keeping to the back roads as much through necessity as prudence. The main thoroughfares were clogged with military traffic as the German army scrambled to maintain its hold in the west and the Allies pressed relentlessly forward.

At Neheim-Husten Ivan used some of his precious Deutschmarks to buy a second bicycle from a schoolteacher who had returned from the front minus a leg and full of bitterness over it. April, after its unpromising start, had turned sunny and warm, and with their extra wheels, Dragan and Ivo made good time, taking turns pulling the wagon.

"Think how fast we could go if we didn't have to keep diving for cover," Dragan said.

The front lay well behind them now but American patrols flew daily sorties across the countryside, targeting anything that moved on the road and regularly forcing the two men into ditches and under trees. By night, they slept in barns. Farmers' sons, and often their daughters, were somewhere else fighting for the Reich. The wrinkled faces that anxiously answered the knock on the door softened in relief when the two young Serbs offered strong backs in exchange for a little food to eat and a hay stack to sleep in.

Hard news was difficult to come by. Newspapers were scarce and the old women willing to share their chicken and potatoes were less willing to discuss the progress of the war. Perhaps they were afraid of jinxing the outcome. Their husbands, their sons, and grandsons were still fighting. Where? They didn't know. For how much longer? They didn't know that either.

As they crested a rise near Brilon, Dragan and Ivan heard the familiar drone of an approaching aircraft.

"Not again," Ivan groaned. "I'm getting to know the ditches around here so well we're practically on a first-name basis."

But even as they braked to a halt and got off their bikes, they heard the plane's engine cough then sputter into silence. Shading his eyes against the glare, Dragan recognized the familiar single star and two stripes of the American air force. The plane hovered weightless for an instant before it began to fall and Dragan felt his own arms grow rigid with the strain of controlling its glide. Half a minute later and less than a kilometre away, it hit the ground.

From their vantage point on the hillside, Dragan and Ivan watched a dazed pilot climb stiffly out of the cockpit and tumble down the side of the plane to the ground. His good luck was short lived. Before he could get his bearings, a swarm of angry villagers surrounded him, eager to vent their hostility on the enemy who had so literally fallen into their clutches.

"It's a lynch mob, for God's sake," Dragan said. "Haven't they ever heard of the Geneva Convention?"

"Doubt they care," Ivan said. "They won't have time to string him up anyway. Look, there's a military truck coming."

They scrambled for cover, laying their bicycles flat on the ground and sliding down the short, steep bank beside them into a screen of bearded grasses and spreading gorse. Heavy, spiked branches of evergreen swept to the ground on three sides but behind them, tree roots only clutched at the bank, allowing Dragan and Ivan to force their way through the tangle into a perfect, though uncomfortable, shelter. Dragan winced as thorns tore his hands and lashed his shoulders. He felt his foot connect with something soft.

There was a low curse in what sounded like Italian.

Amazing, Dragan thought, how many people were roaming the countryside, moving in all directions in a crazy game of musical chairs, where each of them had lost his seat and was desperately trying to find another. They spoke in a polyglot babble, a few words of one language, whole phrases in another. One question was on everyone's lips: when will it be over?

Dragan twisted his neck and saw not one other man but two, hiding in the gorse behind him. The one he had kicked had the broad back and rough hands of a labourer. The thin, fair-haired boy with him had an owlish look that spoke of a softer life.

They lay together in silence until dusk fell and all sounds from the valley had faded away. Then they crawled out from under the bushes and stretched their cramped limbs.

"Where are you from?" the boy asked. He could as easily have asked, Where are you going?" The answer would have been the same.

"Belgrade," Dragan said. "And you?"

"Milan."

"You were at university there?"

The boy nodded. As he was about to say more, his body went rigid and he groaned and moved away.

"He's ill," Dragan said.

"He'll be all right," the older man said, but his face was anxious. "He doesn't like fuss. These attacks hit him every so often — he ate something that keeps turning him inside out."

"He needs rest," Ivan said. "And starch. Feed him potatoes, no seasoning. No dairy."

The boy came back to where the other three waited. He was wiping sweat from his brow with his sleeve. His friend patted him on the shoulder. "We'd better be moving on," he said. He looked at Ivan. "Potatoes, no dairy," he repeated. "I'll remember. In case you haven't heard, over near Kassel the German police are arresting all non-Germans they find wandering around. They're putting them in detention camps."

"What about the Americans? Where are they now?"

"The American Army's already at Frankfurt, and they're

moving north fast — straight for Marburg and Kassel."

That decided it. Dragan and Ivan would head south toward Frankfurt.

They arrived at the village of Osterode on the night of April 13, 1945. The next morning, so did the American army.

AFTERMATH

Germany, 1945–1946

They called us survivors, but none of us survived.
We merely stayed alive.
  — A camp inmate

It was raining when the Americans reached Osterode and
Dragan learned he had been right in predicting that it would
take time for them to sort out who was who in Germany. The MP
who interrogated him spoke only English — the one language
still missing from Dragan's lexicon. He and Ivan were corralled
with several hundred German POWs in a mud-soaked field where
they spent the night asleep on their feet like horses, waking at
intervals shivering and semi-jelled. A strong morning sun eventually warmed them and the MPs who had kept watch all night
went yawning to their quarters while the new officer in charge
asked, this time in German, whether there were any non-Germans in the group. Dragan and Ivan alone stepped forward.

Among the prisoners in the corral was the blustering mayor
of Osterode, a man more used to giving orders than to taking
them. His cheeks reddened but he nodded when the grim-faced
captain in charge told him to find room and board for the two
Serbs, and to make sure they were well taken care of. Dragan
and Ivan went home with a farmer whose son was still fighting in
Russia and whose fields needed ploughing and seeding.

Once the crops were planted, Dragan and Ivan decided to move on. They wandered south, careful to stay behind the American advance until they reached Frankenberg, where they squatted for a few days in an abandoned building. Most of the apartment's furnishings had been removed, but there was still a working stove in the kitchen and few could cook potatoes with as much flair as Dragan.

On May third, several American army transport trucks arrived, gathered up all the foreigners living in the town, added them to their growing collection, and deposited them at a camp near Wetzlar, sixty kilometres south on the river Lahn. In the new euphemism of the time, Dragan had officially become a "displaced person," lacking even the status of a refugee.

Refugees were familiar human by-products of war, residents of combat zones who had been set adrift by the destruction of their homes and their livelihoods. Pitied as individuals, en masse they became a menace, clogging roads, taxing already strained civilian services, and spreading panic and disease. But whatever threat they posed, they were at least a transitory one: in liberated territory, the local authorities were expected to take care of them and in enemy territory, they were compelled to do so.

A displaced person was a different and more complex species altogether. He and his fellows had only two things in common: they were citizens of the United Nations — by definition, enemy aliens no matter where they were found did not qualify as such — and they were outside their national boundaries when they were liberated.

Official policy in regards to these victims of Nazism was that they should be treated for the worst of their physical abuse and then be sent home. Military planners assumed that the DPs' first desire once they realized they were free would be to get away from their German masters and, if possible, get out of Germany to take up their lives where they had left off. They expected their charges to be tractable, grateful, and powerless. But the DPs were none of these things. Many suffered from "liberation complex," a psychological stew that blended revenge with hunger and exultation, three passions that combined to make them as much a problem of behaviour as of care, feeding, disinfection, registration, and repatriation.

For DPs, liberation didn't mark a happy ending to a terrible story; it heralded the start of another harsh struggle. No sooner had they won the fight for physical survival than they were forced to begin a lengthier one to return to life.

Liberated but not free — that was the paradox, Dragan thought. Since the outbreak of war his whole being had been consumed with the hope of staying alive. Now that he was saved, what was there left to hope for?

ii

In 1945 more than twenty million dislocated souls struggled to return to life across the devastated continent. Physically drained, emotionally spent, in a foreign land, and at the mercy of relief organizations, most only wanted to go home. But for many, "home" was a thing of the past — to be enjoyed again only in everlasting nostalgia.

The care and disposition of the DPs was one of the most perplexing issues in postwar Europe. Meagre intelligence and false assumptions about the nature and extent of the problem made it difficult to resolve. Even estimates of the number of people needing help were impossible to make: governments-in-exile had, at times, deliberately exaggerated their numbers in order to persuade the Germans that they had exhausted the supply of slave labour, or to mask the activities of the underground. The question of how many people needed help was complicated by the daunting variety of classes among them: forced labourers, refugees,

POWs, concentration camp inmates — each required special consideration. Then too, there were stateless persons — those who had no governmental allegiance because their national government, Allied or enemy, no longer existed.

Europe was a shambles.

It was unrealistic to expect recently liberated governments to assume, unaided, the huge task of caring for so many displaced people. For six years, the military had controlled all communications, facilities, and supplies on the continent. Now, it had no option but to help local authorities run the reception centres, the supply depots and the transit camps that had been established for all DPs liberated by the Allied advance into Germany.

Before and during the war, Camp 538 at Wetzlar housed a Panzer unit. Its barracks, ten four-storey buildings, accommodated nearly six thousand soldiers. Once the war was over, it offered shelter to twice that number of DPs. Like all postwar camps, it was a model of bureaucratic rigidity, confusion, and Allied bickering, and it was divided into two parts: one for the truly liberated, one for the soon to be re-enslaved. American GIs directed truckloads of the free to the parade square. Their Russian counterparts diverted the rest into a barbed-wire encampment.

Dragan stared at the desperate faces behind the fence while he and Ivan waited their turn outside the administration building. A civilian with a megaphone wandered up and down the line repeating instructions in three languages: "Welcome to DP Centre 538. This camp is managed by the United Nations Relief and Rehabilitation Administration. We hope you will be comfortable here while arrangements are made to return you to your homes. All new arrivals must register inside. Once you have registered, you are free to find your own accommodation."

As he passed, Ivan reached out and tapped the man on the shoulder. "Who are those poor buggers over there behind the wire? Germans?"

The UNRRA official shook his head. "Russians."

Dragan said, "Russians! I thought the Russians were on our side."

"Yeah, they were. But Joe Stalin cut a deal at Yalta. All Russian nationals are being repatriated."

"What if they don't want to go?"

The UNRRA man shrugged. "Too bad."

Months before Germany surrendered, Stalin had made his claims to Eastern Europe plain: Russian spoils of war would include sovereignty over everything east of the Curzon Line and the Soviet occupation zone in Germany. That the division of Germany would mean the division of Europe was clear. Millions of people were about to be abandoned to the will of the Stalinists. In the factory at Ludwigshutte, Nina pointed a shaky finger at the map still hanging on the wall and said, "Look, Heinrich, it's all ours now."

The Americans had been in control for only a week but events moved quickly. The Leningraders were notified they would be transferred to a transit camp prior to being shipped back to their homeland. It didn't take them long to pack. They were loaded into trucks and taken to Wetzlar, where they were sorted by nationality. They were searched and so was their luggage, but the women were lightly passed over and no one noticed that the young Russian girl with the long brown braids was carrying a dagger and a loaded gun. Galina didn't stop to think what would happen if she was caught with the weapons; she only knew she could smuggle them into camp more successfully than Emil. Once safely past the checkpoint, she handed her friend the Luger and kept the knife. Nina and Lily were blissfully unaware she had either.

The Russian compound at Wetzlar was easy to recognize: placards and slogans festooned the walls beside portraits of important comrades. Stalin's picture was the largest. The Leningraders were herded inside a four-storey building, empty except for a scattering of discarded papers. The rooms began to fill quickly as a long line of trucks deposited their human cargo at the door. Looking haggard and depressed, Nina and Lily sank to the floor hugging their knees, their courage finally exhausted.

Galina felt too restless to sit. She wandered out into the corridor and was bowled over by a boy moving fast in the opposite direction. Once they had sorted out the tangle of arms and legs, the boy told her he was from Pulkovo, near Leningrad. Eager for stories of home, Galina encouraged his chatter. She listened in growing dismay as he expounded his plans for the future, the studies he wanted to pursue, and his conviction that Mother Russia needed him now more than ever. Pleading the need for air, Galina fled outside. She stopped abruptly on the doorstep, appalled at the sight of so many sleeves wrapped with the red Party armband. Memory overwhelmed her. The "beauty" of life under the Soviets meant shortages, queues, false history. It meant terror and repression and loss. She felt a sudden urge to run as far and as fast as she could.

But a barbed-wire fence surrounded the compound and two soldiers guarded its gate. The captives on the Russian side stared through the wire at the free zone, praying for help to arrive. Some walked the perimeter searching for weak spots to exploit. Others stared unseeingly into space. Galina noticed that some people moved freely back and forth through the gate, their only identification the coloured paper flags pinned to their chests. They were the paper flags of free nations. She glanced around the courtyard. The Soviet officials were all busy, preparing to celebrate the First of May. They were building a podium, testing the microphone. Galina hurried back to her quarters.

Ten minutes later she emerged again. She walked shoulder to shoulder with Nina and Lily. They carried their suitcases and wore small paper flags pinned to their coats. They marched boldly to the gate, then faltered under the piercing stare of the Russian soldier who stood on one side of it. Galina drew a deep breath and turned to the American standing opposite. She pointed to the little red and white flag on her lapel. In halting English she said, "Poland. We from Poland."

The GI looked from the lovely girl with her hair still in pigtails to the tired, frightened faces of the two women beside her. Smiling a little, he said, "Sure, honey, I get you. You're Polish. You don't belong in here. Okay. You and the grandmas can go ahead, march right on through. We'll get you registered on the other side." He glanced over at the Russian, who studiously avoided eye contact. "Nobody's going to stop you."

iii

Dragan and Ivan found a small, unoccupied space in an attic and staked out sleeping quarters with the blankets they had brought with them from Selbeck. There were only a few of their countrymen among the thousands of French, Dutch, Belgians, and Poles who filled the camp, and the western Europeans were quickly repatriated. Within a few weeks of Dragan's arrival, the majority of the DPs still at Wetzlar were Poles.

Camp populations shifted with the tide of refugees moving across Europe, and communities developed there as they did anywhere else. People fell in love, got married, had children. Men seduced women and wives left their husbands. Lawyers' briefcases bulged with other people's problems. Knives flashed in brawls over space; doctors sewed up the losers. Rival newspapers covered camp elections with impassioned fury. New businesses emerged: barber and cobbler shops, tailors, ersatz lemonade stands, and beer gardens. Even the clothing distribution centres were set up like department stores, with a men's, a women's, and a children's section, and a curtained dressing room where the charity garments could be tried on before selection. There was a lot of time and little to fill it with but sport. In some camps, soccer and volleyball games ran almost nonstop.

Ivan had become leader of the Yugoslav community. As his assistant and interpreter, Dragan helped find accommodation and food for new arrivals, who continued to flood through the camp gates. It wasn't long before they started organizing dances in the hall where, only a few months before, German officers had taken their meals.

May 8 was celebrated in Camp 538 as it was all over Europe, with music and dancing. The band was a group of Yugoslav officers who were freed POWs. After VE Day they played at a lot of dances at the camp, which Dragan enjoyed even more than he did soccer games. He was light on his feet, a smooth talker, and he had enough self-assurance to approach any young lady he fancied. He had just finished a waltz with a particularly lissom blonde when he looked across the room and fell in love.

iv

Laughing and breathless, Galina and Genya collapsed into chairs. Genya took off a shoe and started to massage her foot.

"I think my toes are ready to fall off." She waggled them experimentally. "Do you think I could dance barefoot?"

"I don't know. There are a lot of left feet stomping around out there."

"Well, there's at least one fellow who knows how to move his feet and he keeps looking right at you. He's cute, don't you think?"

Galina wrinkled her nose. "Too aggressive. He was smiling at me when I was dancing with Ciro. And I don't like the gap in his teeth."

The music started again and Genya tried to squeeze her swollen foot back into her shoe.

"Excuse me. Would you care to dance?"

Galina looked up. The gap-toothed young man stood in front of her holding out his hand, his smile telling her he was sure of her acceptance.

"Thank you, no. I prefer to sit this one out."

Something flickered in the young man's eyes and was gone before Galina could decipher what it meant. Her mouth suddenly felt dry. Genya looked at her curiously. The young man bowed. "Perhaps another time," he said, and moved away.

"Wow," said Genya.

Galina set her jaw. "I told you, too aggressive. But now what am I supposed to do? I turned him down. I can't very well go and dance with someone else."

She sat forlornly on the sidelines while Genya waltzed off in the arms of a young Polish officer. The whirling couples and lively music had her tapping her foot impatiently, waiting for the dance to end and the next to begin. She looked around for Ciro, finally spotting him on the far side of the room. He held a glass of lemonade in each hand and he was trying to thread his way through the traffic jam on the floor without spilling any. He caught her eye, signalling she should stay where she was. She smiled and nodded.

"Does this mean you'll dance with me this time?" Galina's heart sank. It was the gap-toothed Serb again, irritatingly persistent. Was he determined to spoil her evening?

There was a sudden commotion among the dancers. Galina heard the sharp, unmistakable slap of flesh against flesh and someone cursed loudly in Italian. In spite of his best efforts, Ciro's careful progress across the room had been interrupted by a young lady practicing a twirl. Her outflung arm had caught him full across the face, sending him stumbling backwards. Automatically, he had raised his hands to protect himself and dropped the lemonade, which splashed over shoes and trouser cuffs in an arcing spray. The result was predictable. Like a genie popping suddenly from a bottle, pent-up frustrations erupted in a sea of fists and fingernails. Dragan took a few steps forward as though he intended to join the mêlée and then thought better of it. He had seen all this before. He turned back to Galina with a witty comment on his lips, only to find she had disappeared.

γ

As soon as the fight broke out, Galina seized her chance to escape. It was a shame to have such a promising evening ruined, but if she left now there was a good chance the "annoyance" wouldn't notice until she was well out the door. With any luck, she wouldn't run into him again.

She paused in the yellow circle of light outside the door. Beyond it stretched the dark expanse of the soccer field. The building she lived in lay in a straight line on the far side. She could see a dim glow in a few of the windows and knew that hers was among those still lit. Nina never went to bed before her daughter came home. It was part of the fun, telling Mama and Tante who was wearing what and who was dancing with whom. Mostly, of course, they wanted to know who was dancing with her.

The night was warm but a fresh breeze was stirring and Galina wrapped her sweater more tightly around her shoulders before stepping into the darkness. She'd only taken a few steps when she stumbled on the uneven ground, twisting her ankle. Galina groaned. It wasn't a bad sprain, but she'd be more comfortable barefoot than in heels. The soccer pitch was swept regularly so there weren't likely to be any large pebbles there to stub her toes on. Shoeless, she walked on as quickly as her footing and the darkness would allow, keeping her eyes fixed on the dim glow that marked her destination.

Inside the hall, the band struck up a polka. Hearing the music, Galina wondered if that meant the fists had stopped flying or if the tune was merely lending rhythm to the punches. She hummed along, hardly noticing when the music surged more loudly for a moment and then muted as the door to the hall opened and closed. It was only when the polka ended that she heard the footsteps behind her.

Galina paused, half turning. "Genya?" She really ought to have told her friend she was leaving. Not that it would have made any difference; Genya never left a party before it was over. There was a note of uncertainty in Galina's voice when she repeated, "Genya?"

No answer. The steady footsteps drew nearer. Sensing a masher, Galina clutched her shoes tightly to her chest and began to run. She had nearly reached the edge of the field when she felt the air move behind her. She shrieked and whirled to face her attacker.

"A gentleman always sees a lady home," Dragan said.

vi

"Galuchka, I don't understand you. Why won't you see this Dragan? He moons around here all the time, waiting for you to throw him a crumb."

"I thought it was you he was coming to see. You're the one he brings the cigarettes for. I don't like him. He scared me to death that night at the dance, creeping up behind me like that. Anyway, he's too old for me."

"Old? Mature. Not like those boys you hang around with. That Beppe, for one. I've heard he likes to drive a motorcycle down the main street of Wetzlar holding a stick out the window so he can trip all the Germans and break their legs. Is that what you want in a man?"

Galina sighed. How could she explain to her mother that she didn't want a man, not any man, really. Not to marry and settle down. It was more fun being the lollipop in the candy store. She enjoyed the love letters, the gifts, the signed photos she collected as she had once collected the souvenir booklets at the cinema. Dragan had his role in her fantasy: he was the faithful but rejected suitor trying to storm the walls of Palazzo Q.

Palazzo Q was a joke. In order to maintain the fiction that they were Polish citizens, Nina, Galina, and Lily had adopted Polish names and moved into the Polish "neighbourhood." They now occupied a stall in what had once been a pig barn. All buildings in the camp had letter designations. The pig barn was Q. Palazzo was an embellishment suggested by Ciro in honour of the relative elegance of the structure. Agriculture being much more advanced in Germany than elsewhere in Europe, the two-storey barn boasted tiled floors and plenty of windows. The Leningraders-cum-Poles had a private stall all to themselves. During the day they left the top half of the Dutch door open so they could watch the comings and goings of their neighbours.

One morning a man knocked on the door and asked Nina a question. She shook her head. He asked again, a little louder. Since language, not deafness, was the problem, Nina still couldn't help him. She had learned a few Polish words, but the similarity to Russian was more confusing than helpful as she'd found when someone asked to borrow her iron and she'd offered up a piece of tin. Now she could only smile and nod, palms up in the universal sign for "I haven't got a clue." "*Spaseba,*" the man said and turned away. Nina heard a clunk of wood, some shuffling in the straw, and nothing more. It was perhaps three hours later that she discovered what the man had been asking. Two boys slept in the dovecote and they kept a ladder propped against the wall as a staircase. The man had asked who the ladder belonged to. Because Nina couldn't tell him, he assumed it was available to anyone. So he had taken it, leaving the boys without access to their home. Serious post-war diplomacy in the form of cigarettes had been needed to resolve the issue.

vii

Dutch, French, Belgians, and Italians were the first to be repatriated. Soon after, most of the Serbs also left Wetzlar, first for Munich, then Pangau and finally, Yugoslavia, where Tito had established his Communist satellite state. Dragan wavered. He was anxious to go home, to find his family and let them know he was still alive. He'd had no contact with them for more than two years, not since the day he'd been arrested in the Belgrade marketplace. He was curious to see if the new Yugoslavia could really become the heaven on earth he had dreamed of. But he didn't want to go back alone. Galina obsessed him. He wanted nothing more than to bring her home and show her off; what better way to prove himself as a man than to win such a wife? As long as she stayed in Wetzlar, so would he. Ivan, too, decided to stay for reasons of the heart and his affair with an UNRAA official provided the unexpected bonus of a new job for Dragan, which he sorely needed after an incident in the registration office.

The rules for being admitted to a DP camp were clear: enemy aliens did not qualify, though many tried. And why not? Camp conditions might be far from ideal but at the very least they guaranteed food, shelter, and medical attention. The same could hardly be said for the rest of the country. Across the length and breadth of Germany, people scrabbled in the ruins of their shattered cities and cratered farmlands wondering which evil would strike them down first: looters, starvation, or typhus.

Disputes arose over nationality, particularly in cases of intermarriage. But with UNRAA resources already stretched to the breaking point, the rules had to be followed as they had been laid down. Dragan saw no reason to make an exception for an ex-Wehrmacht soldier with a non-German wife. According to the law, the woman became a German citizen when she married, which meant it was that government's job to take care of the couple. From behind his desk, Dragan pointed to the door. The Wehrmacht captain hurled abuse that grew progressively louder the closer he shuffled to the exit.

"Serb bastard!" he finally spat.

Dragan felt a quick, hot spurt of anger. Loathing gripped him so strongly it felt like a physical illness. This man was the enemy who had invaded his country, murdered his people, and turned him into a slave. What did he, what did anyone, owe him and his kind now? Still, Dragan was careful to steady his voice. "You'll be entitled to a place in this camp when hair grows on the palm of my hand," he said.

The German swung at him and Dragan felt his anger grow. It worked its way up from the pit of his stomach to spread along his back and his shoulders and down the length of his arms. He was surprised by the weight of it. He thought, "I'd like to kill this man."

Two coworkers grabbed him and hauled him away before he could give in to the temptation.

His supervisor, a patrician-looking woman from Virginia, counselled him against the evils of racism and UNRAA issued him an official letter of reprimand. Two weeks later, the German and his wife were admitted to Camp 538; its soccer team was in desperate need of a strong right forward.

Dragan moved to the soft goods warehouse, where his literacy and bookkeeping skills proved invaluable.

The mandate of the UN Relief and Rehabilitation Administration was to provide quick, efficient, and effective aid to territories ravaged by the war. Countries that had been lucky enough to escape devastation pooled their resources to send food, medicine, clothing, and other emergency materials to those in need. Controlling the resulting flow of supplies became a complex exercise in logistics. Tons of goods were now being shipped into Germany and every parcel had to be opened and its contents sorted. All foodstuffs were turned over to the camp kitchens. Cigarettes were stored in the warehouse and distributed once a week: they were, as ever, prime bargaining chips. Though he wasn't a smoker himself, Dragan recognized the value of cigarettes in trade and he made sure he always had some when he visited Palazzo Q. If he couldn't win Galina by direct attack, he was not averse to winning her through her mother.

Dragan was permitted to move out of the camp and into the town of Wetzlar. The space he found to live in was no larger than what he left behind, but it was a step toward a more normal life — outside a gated enclosure rather than in. He rented the living room of a three-bedroom apartment in a building that housed the families of German officers. His landlady, Frau Menke, didn't know when, or if, her husband would return. He was a prisoner of war somewhere in Russia. She and her three small children crowded into a single bedroom so that the other two could be let, one to a lady doctor from the camp, the other to a Jewish woman. Both had been at Dachau. Here was the war in a nutshell, Dragan thought, the damning and the damned together, and all facing ruin, loss, and a constant shortage of food.

Dragan's paycheque and connections helped supplement the larder and Frau Menke did all the cooking. At night Dragan slept on the sofa and dreamed about Galina; by day he sat at his desk in the warehouse and thought about her. The last time he had tried to see her, she had ignored him completely and gone for walk with her Dutch friend Peter. Dragan felt a knot of pain in his stomach when he thought of it. He stared out the window and watched the afternoon sky slowly darken over Palazzo Q.

viii

She accepted him finally, as Emil would have said, faute de mieux. No one had made a better offer. One by one Galina's suitors had melted away, repatriated to their homes in France, and Italy, and Holland, and none had invited her to follow. Romance had been as much a game to them as it was to her, a pleasant interlude of moonlit trysts and violin serenades that held no promise for the future. Dragan was the rock on which she could build a new life. But even as he issued his ultimatum — marry me or I return to Yugoslavia — Galina had no real understanding of what it meant to be a wife. All she knew was this handsome young Serb had already become a fixture, in her life and her mother's, with his flattery, flowers, and cigarettes. The idea of losing him was upsetting. So she said yes. If the luck that had brought them this far held, love might come later.

They plighted their troth on a hill overlooking the Lahn. They sat on the grass amid the green-gold of buds turning quickly to leaf, the muddy ground beyond them drying to friable earth, the river shimmering as it flowed ceaselessly forward. Dragan took in a deep lungful of air. The sense of having her next to him, her shoulder touching his, her warm breath on his cheek, was righter than he could ever have imagined. He had little faith left in God or man. His greatest accomplishment in life had been to survive. But now, having won the girl of his dreams, he felt buoyant and strange, as if something heavy was missing. As if he had finally set something down.

Nina was entertaining some friends to tea when Galina threw open the door of Palazzo Q and gaily announced, "I'm getting married in June."

The neighbours were all agog. Nina just smiled. "That's nice," she said. "We can talk about it later."

There wasn't much to say; Nina wouldn't interfere with her

daughter's choice. Her own marriage to Sergei had been a disappointment grudgingly borne by her family, their attitude slightly softened by their own years of ostracism when Peter married Paraskeva. In those days, the world had turned differently. Now, social status and family name, the cornerstones on which futures had once been built, no longer counted for much. The steadfast air and strong hands of the worker had become the only currency with which one could guarantee another day of life. Nina wouldn't sanction return to a Communist country but, now that he'd won his prize, Dragan happily focussed on Canada. Two years later, Galina and Dragan, Nina and Lily boarded a ship at Cherbourg and crossed the ocean the wartime mystic in Kropotkin had foreseen.

Whatever they had once imagined the future to be, time and circumstance had altered those dreams. And chance had seen them through.

POSTSCRIPT

Some of the displaced did eventually return home. But many, like Dragan and Galina, recognized the political and economic changes taking place in Europe and used their displacement as a chance to emigrate. During the war the DPs had been forced to leave their homelands and go to work for a totalitarian regime. Afterward they struggled to build themselves a niche in a new country. Their immediate goals were no different than those of others who had survived the war: a regular income, an apartment or house, a car. But for many, the work they had done for the Nazis was their only qualification for a job. That dreadful experience was the only experience they had.

People who had lost everything now scrambled to get their papers and their new lives in order. They tackled huge psychological barriers in learning a new language and a new culture. They faced bigotry and racism, homesickness and grief. But these difficulties were nothing compared to the isolation the immigrants felt in their new land.

And what of the places they came from?

Dragan returned to Yugoslavia several times after the war. On his first visit, his mother took him to the school in Petrinja where his name had been engraved alongside those of so many others lost in the war. On his second, he took his son Sergei with him and the Canadian boy danced at a *berba* with his Serb and

Croat cousins. But in the closing years of the twentieth century, Dragan saw his homeland ripped apart by a civil war as vicious and devastating as the one he had witnessed decades before. Ethnic grievances effectively held in check by the Communist dictator Tito exploded when he died: the country of Dragan's birth now no longer exists.

Galina returned to Russia only after the collapse of Communism. The apartment building she lived in is slowly settling back into the marshes St. Petersburg sprang from and she had to descend a few steps in order to get in the front door. Sixty-five years after the first bullets were fired, the scars of German shells are still visible on the walls.

Razhivatka has disappeared. After the war, the Soviets demolished the *stanitsa*. Its entire population was either shot or sent to Siberia.

The labour camps in Germany are gone too, but many of the companies they supported, including Krupp and Buderus, still survive.

Galina, 1946

Dragan, 1946

Dragan and Galina, newly engaged.

194

Nina and Sergei a few years before his arrest.

Heiratsurkunde

(Standesamt — — — — — — — — — — M e t z l a r — — — — — — — Nr. 245/1946. II

Der Lehrer Dragutin M e t i k o s c h , orthodox — — — — — — — —
— — — — — — — — — , wohnhaft in M e t z l a r , Scharnhorststraße 3 — — ,
geboren am 31. August 1920 — — — in Biele Vode/Jugoslawien — — — — — — —

(Standesamt — Nr. — — — — —), und

die Krankenschwester Halina J a n o w s k a , orthodox — — — — — —
— — — — — — — , wohnhaft in M e t z l a r , Scharnhorststraße 3 — — —
geboren am 29. April 1927 — — — in B r o d y /Polen — — — — — — — — —

(Standesamt — Nr. — — — — —),

haben am 12. J u n i 1946 — — — — — — — — — — — — — vor dem Standesamt

M e t z l a r — die Ehe geschlossen.

B 151. Heiratsurkunde (mit Elternangabe)
Verlag für Standesamtswesen G.m.b.H., Berlin SW 61, Gitschiner Str. 109. (f. 14) C/1431

B 151

The marriage licence issued to Dragan and Galina. To avoid repatriation to Russia, Galina assumed a Polish name. The licence was corrected years later, from the safety of Canada.

196

Main gate, DP Camp 538, Wetzlar. The camp was run by the United Nations Relief and Rehabilitation Administration (UNRRA).

Galina's home in Wetzlar, a former pigsty nicknamed "Palazzo Q."

197

Acknowledgements

I would like to thank my husband, Serge, for inspiring me to begin *Chance,* and my friend, the poet Anna Mioduchowska, for encouraging me to finish it.

Anne Metikosh, daughter-in-law to Dragan and Galina, was born in Montreal and raised in Toronto. A former resident of Sudbury, Yellowknife, Halifax, and Burlington, she and her family currently make Calgary their home. Anne's writing has been featured in several anthologies, including *Beginnings* and *Chicken Soup for the Parent's Soul*. She has also published a young-adult historical fiction title, *Terra Incognita,* and a mystery novel, *Undercurrent.*

The text face is set in ITC Veljovic, a typeface designed by the Yugoslavian calligrapher Jovica Veljovic in 1984. The "letters to the front" are set in ITC Esprit, also designed by Veljovic in 1985. The accompanying script face is Ex Ponto, designed by Veljovic in 1995, and it is based on the rhythm of his handwriting.